SEAN F

GET OFF
YOUR DUFF
AND MAKE YOUR
OWN @#$! CHEESE

**It's up to YOU to make
things happen for yourself**

Get Off Your Duff and
Make Your Own @#$! Cheese

ISBN: 1479182532
ISBN 13: 9781479182534

Book Design and Art Direction: Dianne Kehoe
Illustration: Meaghan Kehoe

TESTIMONIALS

"'We need to steer clear of this poverty of ambition, where people want to drive fancy cars and wear nice clothes and live in nice apartments but don't want to work hard to accomplish these things. Everyone should try to realize their full potential'. I said that in 2005 and believe Sean is saying the same thing in his book. It's time for change so get off your duff."
– President of the United States, Barack Obama

"It's very possible that this story is about you. If so, and you don't like what you see, then as this book says, get off your duff and do something about it. Why? Because you can indeed change your life dramatically. But only if YOU change first. In the end, it's always the person who gives first, and gives more, that wins in so many ways."
– Brett McFall, Australia's Expert At Making Online Business Easy

"Sean Roach is here not to impress you but impress upon you that when you Pour Your Heart Into It, you D.A.R.E to be fulfilled."
– Howard Schultz, Chairman and CEO of Starbucks

"Powerful, insightful and focused. This book is a must read for anyone that wants to get the most out of life. Great motivation to give you the mindset to get done what needs to be done! Never confuse activity with productivity! I recommended it to my entire team."
– Chad B., Naval Aviator

"If more people did what Sean says in this book, the world would be a different place!"
– Andre Agassi, the Andre Agassi Charitable Foundation

"If you are in a rut, this book will motivate you to get on track! It's amazing how much your life changes when you change how you look at your life! I now realize the importance of following my dreams and my goals, no matter what life 'throws' at you! This book got me fired up!!!"
– Angela M, Flight Attendant

"I LUV the title of your book! I am honored and humbled that you would include me in your book."
– Colleen Barrett, Former President and Corporate Secretary of Southwest Airlines

"I wish I had this book along time ago. Get off your Duff made me realize the importance of following your dreams, regardless of what the people around you think you should be doing with your life."
– John A., Chiropractor

"It's an inspiring collection of people, like myself, who have worked hard, believed they could do it and are excited about the prospects."
– Richard Branson, Chairman of Virgin Group

"Sean uses humor to get a very important message across, related to a good work attitude. Your life will change – if you D.A.R.E. it to. Powerful little book with a powerful message. Easy reading for all ages."
– Dania A, Energy Healing Practitioner

"Sean Roach portrays a philosophy I truly believe in–one cannot neglect change or believe it takes luck to be successful for they risk being disappointed."
– H.H. Sheikh Mohammad Bin Rashid Al Maktoum, Vice President and Prime Minister of the UAE, and Ruler of Dubai

"On Sean Roach's book, it crept up on me then 'slap', it kinda hurt, then I got off my duff and started taking action steps. Powerful!"
– Georg G, Owner of Katalyst Marketing

"The success of a company isn't based on money but the people you have running it. More employees need to appreciate the perspective outlined in this book!
– Steve Jobs, Co-founder, Chairman, CEO of Apple Inc

"Uplifting and encouraged me to act on a few things right away. Thank you Sean Roach. This book has a very positive affect on my life/ job. I know of a few friends and family members who I will be buying this for (cause I love them)."

– Connie A. Teacher

"It's hard work getting rich! Everyone in this book is living proof of that! That's the lesson people will take away from this book."

– Gene Simmons, Entrepreneur and Co-founder of Kiss

To my parents,
Larry and Ruby

ACKNOWLEDGMENTS

Many years of thought and action went into the creation of this book. Firstly, I need to express my sincerest gratitude to my family, especially my mother, Ruby, and father, Larry. Thank you for teaching me to believe in my potential and that if anything is going to happen, it's up to me to make it happen.

To Pia, my fiancée, thank you for your love, encouragement and support throughout my endeavors. Thank you for being there to share my thoughts and ideas.

Although I'm involved in many charities, I would like to give a special thanks to Big Brothers Big Sisters of America and San Diego where I'm a board member. What this organization does to get people off their duffs and help children and the communities they live in is amazing. I hope more people give and get involved in any charity. Just Get Off Your Duff and help out!

Last but not least, to my friends and colleagues (there are too many to list, but you know who you are) who took the time to listen, guide and mentor me in my journey throughout this project and, in some cases, my life.

Your words of wisdom and honesty are always greatly appreciated.

ABOUT THE AUTHOR

Over the past decade, Sean Roach has built an entrepreneurial empire helping people grow their businesses. Using his expertise in Internet marketing, organizational turnaround and accessing the right people for success, he provides practical advice on how individuals and businesses can expand their reach and how they can learn to move with inevitable changes in business and technology. As well as major global companies he is bound by confidentiality agreements not to mention, Sean has worked with the likes of MGM, Subaru, BMW, Ford, Coldwell Banker and Century 21.

Sean splits his time between Las Vegas and San Diego and is active within charitable organizations such as Big Brothers Big Sisters of America where he serves on San Diego's board of directors. Since building his career as an entrepreneur, corporate speaker, author and founder/CEO of social networking site GotAccess.com, he has received many accolades from throughout the US and around the world. Sean has been honored with 'Sean Roach Day' from the Mayor of Las Vegas twice, 'Entrepreneur Day' by the Mayors of Raleigh and Carey, North Carolina, and was awarded a proclamation declaring January 17 'Entrepreneur Day' by the Governor of Nevada in Sean's honor.

As a sought-after speaker, Sean shares his knowledge with corporations across a wide range of industries on tangible tactics anyone can use to help them achieve success in their endeavors. In *Get Off Your Duff and Make Your Own @#$! Cheese*, Sean aims to inspire readers to take action and make their goals a reality by giving them the tools to do just that.

INTRODUCTION

If you read books, attend seminars or watch television programs, you will be exposed to a gamut of excuses that explain why people fail to reach their full potential. Below are a number of common reasons provided:

- **Fear of failure**
- **Doubt**
- **Lack of confidence**
- **Pride**
- **Low self-esteem**
- **Arrogance**
- **Self-pity**
- **Hyperactivity**
- **Apathy**
- **Attention Deficit Disorder**
- **Bad advice**
- **Ignorance**
- **Childhood trauma**
- **Adult trauma**
- **General trauma**
- **Lack of trauma**
- **Getting too much love**
- **Getting too little love**
- **A broken heart**
- **A broken spirit**

- **A broken body**
- **Bad relationships**
- **Rejection**
- **Discrimination**
- **Discouragement**
- **Confusion**
- **Shyness**
- **Laziness**
- **Being too nice**
- **Being too rude**
- **Being too rich**
- **Being too poor**
- **Being too skinny**
- **Being too fat**
- **Being too good looking**
- **Being too ugly**
- **Self-hatred**
- **Guilt**
- **Indecisiveness**

And on and on and on it goes. Although there are many excuses which can be used for explaining why someone has failed to reach his or her full potential, the solutions are simple ... so simple, in fact, that they can all be explained in a simple tale about two rats named Pep and Rally.

Get Off Your Duff and Make Your Own @#$! Cheese is the story of two rats who don't simply adjust to change, they learn to make change happen. This is a different kind of change. It involves change to behavioral patterns ways of thinking and the choices we make in our lives.

Pep and Rally have sampled a lot of cheese in their lifetimes, but have grown dissatisfied with simply trying different cheeses. Instead of waiting around for others to supply them with cheese, Pep and Rally decide it is time they make their own cheese. To reach this goal, they need to learn about the cheese-making business. And the best place to learn about making cheese is at the Little Cheese Company.

After securing jobs at the Little Cheese Company, the rats are offered plenty of experience and opportunity. But Pep and Rally become complacent. They begin to enjoy the routine and benefits of working at the Little Cheese Company. In the process, they lose sight of their goals and become overly comfortable.

When Big Cheese Incorporated announces that it is going to buy the Little Cheese Company and downsize its workforce, Pep and Rally aren't worried. But the rats soon find themselves out of work and unable to find jobs in another cheese factory and their dreams of making their own cheese seem like a distant memory. It isn't until a generous friend shares her wisdom that they are able to get excited about life again and make things happen for themselves.

In the following pages, you will recognize many of the situations Pep and Rally face. You will read about the lessons they learn on their life path and you may even relate to the traps that keep the rats from reaching their full potential. More importantly, you will learn to dream your dreams, act on your dreams and realize your true potential.

Through the adventures of Pep and Rally, you will be better equipped to recognize and seize the opportunities that will allow you to achieve that true potential. You will become empowered to open doors to the most productive, rewarding and exciting experiences life has to offer you. In short, you will learn to *Get off Your Duff and Make Your Own @#$! Cheese.*

Making your own cheese doesn't have to mean you become an entrepreneur and take on the world with your own business. Pep and Rally's story shows it is just as rewarding to be the best employee you can possibly be. Not only will you quickly be recognized as a shining star that stands out from others, there's no telling how far you'll go when you're striving to reach your true potential.

I wonder how many of the major corporations going under in the current financial crisis would have survived and even thrived if the philosophy of more of their employees was to do their absolute best and give it their all. What kinds of innovations are companies missing out on by employing workers who do the bare minimum for their pay and think they owe nothing more than that to the companies for which they work? I wonder what cars would look like these days if assembly line workers didn't see themselves as assembly line workers punching in, doing their jobs and punching out again, but as ideas people capable of making safer cars that were smoother to drive.

It's evident how differently a company can perform when its employees want to do their best and are empowered to do so. Consider the different approaches of United Airlines and Singapore Airlines. Flight attendants on United Airlines are assigned to the much-coveted long-haul flights based on seniority – how long they have been with the company. In contrast, Singapore Airlines selects its long-haul flight attendants by using a point system based on compliments and complaints received from passengers. Which airline do you think has better service? On a recent United Airlines flight I was on, a fellow passenger pressed his call bell six times within the space of an hour. No one came.

1

A BRILLIANT IDEA

For those who haven't met them, Pep is a grey rat with a pointy nose and whiskers. Rally is also a grey rat with a pointy nose and whiskers. Actually, he looks pretty much like Pep. Most creatures, especially those who aren't rats themselves, cannot tell them apart.

But Pep and Rally aren't like most rats, or people for that matter. Most people become so caught up in the sources of cheese that they never take time to learn how to create their own cheese. They stay right where they are until all the cheese is gone.

Like people, most rats in Pep and Rally's world apply their intellect, emotions and beliefs to their search for cheese. Once they find cheese, they are satisfied with that cheese. They don't care if it's camembert or cheddar or whether it comes from a cow, goat or ewe. Cheese is cheese and, once they find it, most sit down and eat the cheese until it's gone, at which point they are forced to look for more cheese.

Pep and Rally are passionate about cheese, however. They don't just like it; they adore it. They absolutely, positively, most assuredly *LOVE* cheese. They don't just love one or two kinds of cheese; they love every kind of cheese. And they love cheese on all occasions, whether for dinner, lunch, midnight snack or even breakfast. They love it on crackers, on toast, on apples, even cheese on cheese. They love cheese with wine, with whisky, with water; they even love it with milk.

"Hey, Rally," says Pep. "We absolutely adore cheese, right?"

"Right," says Rally.

"Well, if we love it so much, then we should make it our vocation. We should change our lives so that cheese is a part of each and every day," says Pep.

"Then why don't we make our own @#$! cheese?" they shout in unison.

As you can see, Pep came up with the idea that they should make their own cheese. He is the rat with innovative ideas and is ready to pursue them with no further thought. Rally is more calculating. He considers Pep's ideas, often likes them, but wants to ensure they are savvy rats who don't jump into anything without thinking it through. This is why the two friends begin to explore all there is to know about cheese.

Each day, when they finish work at the car wash where they met, they head off to do their research. They begin by taking a good, long sniff of all the different cheeses they encounter, making notes and comparing vintages before savoring each mouth-watering bite. They track down experts and quiz them on the finer points of cheese and scurry through libraries in search of knowledge.

After one exhausting day of study, the rats settle down to contemplate their findings.

"We know a lot about cheese now, right?" said Rally.

"A whole lot about it," Pep agreed.

"You think we're ready?" Rally asked.

"I suppose so," Pep said, gnawing through a rind of brie.

"It has to be a special cheese," Rally said.

"Yep, one no one else has done before," Pep said.

Pep grinned at Rally and Rally grinned at Pep.

They were so confident they now knew enough about cheese to be able to come up with the perfect flavor, texture and aroma that they felt sure their cheese would be a raging success. Pep smiled, thinking of the possibilities. They would be rich. They could eat whatever cheese they wanted, whenever they wanted, however they wanted. They would be known as the rats who got off their duffs to make their own @#$! cheese.

While Pep was having these lofty fantasies, Rally examined the packaging of the round of brie Pep had just demolished.

"Hey, Pep," he said.

"Huh?" Pep answered dreamily.

"Do you know how they make these rounds? How they rind? I mean, not in theory, but at the production plant? Do you know how much the equipment costs to make them? How many people need to be hired? How you get the cheese to market?"

Pep looked perplexed, "Um…"

Rally looked at his claws. "Hey, Pep."

"Yeah?"

"What do we really know about the actual production, distribution and marketing of cheese?"

"We know all about cheese," Pep said defensively.

"Yeah, but what do we know about *making* cheese?" Rally said.

Pep stared at Rally.

Rally stared at Pep.

They looked away in unison.

In silence, they each reviewed the situation. They knew the taste, texture and smell of cheeses A to Z, but they had no experience actually making cheese. They could read books, take classes and they could watch television programs all about how cheese was made but none of this was enough to realize their dream of making their own cheese.

"We could Google it," Pep said.

"Where's that going to get us?" Rally asked.

Pep frowned, grabbed the packaging from Rally and looked at it closely — it still held a faint whiff off that delicious brie. "Brought to you by Papa Fromage and Sons," he read.

"I've got it!" Pep shouted.

"What?"

"We should get a job at a cheese factory!" Pep said.

Rally nodded. "We could learn a lot about making cheese by working in a cheese factory."

"Let's go!" they shouted.

And so they did, right away, lickety-slip, without wasting time, and applied for jobs at The Little Cheese Company.

Pep and Rally have set a goal for themselves. It is a goal they are passionate about, and something they have put a lot of thought into. They put together a plan to achieve their goal and are eager to get started. Their first step is to work at The Little Cheese Factory. What is your first step to reach your goal and true potential? You can read more stories about people who have achieved their goals by working for others and being the best employees they can be at www.MakeYourOwnDamnCheese.com. You can also submit a story about a job you held that helped you gain the skills and expertise to Get Off Your Duff, or you can submit a story of someone you know that has done just that. Every week we are picking a story, and if we pick your story you, or both you and the person you tell us about will win great prizes.

2

LEARNING AT THE LITTLE CHEESE COMPANY

The Little Cheese Company made specialty cheeses, quality cheeses and cheeses you may never have even heard of. When it came to learning about how to make cheese, Pep and Rally could think of no better factory than The Little Cheese Company and were thrilled to be offered work there.

All the vice presidents of The Little Cheese Company were impressed that Pep and Rally knew so much about cheese. In fact, the VPs of The Little Cheese Company were so impressed that they offered Pep and Rally positions as auditors of the whole company.

Pep and Rally could not think of a better job for learning how to make their own @#$! cheese. They wouldn't have to start at the bottom, sweeping cheese crumbs off the factory floor. As auditors, they would become familiar with all the different departments in a cheese company right from the start. They could ask questions about the business of manufacturing cheese, about how to distribute cheese, market cheese and sell it. They would learn what kind of equipment they needed, how to set up their cheese-making plant and how many employees they would need. They were on their way to becoming not only cheese connoisseurs but also master cheese makers who knew exactly how to get their cheese out to the market.

Week One

On the first day of work, Rally woke up half-an-hour early to make sure traffic wouldn't hinder his early arrival at The Little Cheese Company. When he arrived, Pep was already there to greet him. Pep had gotten up 45 minutes earlier and had beaten Rally by nearly 20 minutes.

A smiling receptionist led the rats to their new office on the third floor before leaving them to make themselves at home.

"How do you like our new office?" Pep asked, holding open the door.

Rally went in, sat at his desk and spun around in his chair.

"This is great," he said.

"Let's get to work!" they said in unison.

The Little Cheese Company was big on training. The company wanted all of its employees to understand the business, their jobs and how everyone worked together. Pep and Rally were given a tour of the plant. They met the other team members: Harry, Irene, Jonathan, Kristen and Leslie. They met for hours with the Creature Resources Department and were handed employee manuals as well as manuals for each department they would be auditing. They were so swamped with information that Pep and Rally kept reading through their lunch break while eating the cheese sandwiches they had brought from home.

When they came to the section titled 'Giving Back', Pep read the first paragraph in delight.

The Little Cheese Company offers many benefits to team members, including complimentary lunches in the cafeteria and ...

"Hey, look here," Pep said through a mouthful. "We get free lunches in the cafeteria."

"Great!" Rally said. "Now I won't have to waste time in the morning making a sandwich. I can head straight to work as soon as I'm ready."

"Free lunch tomorrow!" they said in unison, before burying their heads back in their manuals.

With that, Pep skipped to the next section of the manual. If he had kept reading the 'Giving Back' section to the end, he would have also read:

The Little Cheese Company offers many benefits to team members, including complimentary lunches in the cafeteria and company picnics. In return for these benefits, we ask team members to give back to their communities. You will find a suggestion list detailing some possible ways to give back posted in the break room. We encourage you to add to this list when you hear of opportunities to help.

When Rally reached the section titled 'Giving Back', he skipped it all together. He was more interested in the health plan and the holidays the company observed.

When 5:00pm came, Pep and Rally were still buried in their manuals. Pep didn't finish reading his manual until 6:45pm. By that time his eyes hurt and he was feeling hungry. He looked up just as someone passed by their door.

"Hey, Rally?"

"What, Pep?"

"I think I just saw a beaver walk by."

"A beaver?" Rally said.

"What's a beaver doing in a cheese factory?" they asked in unison.

They would find out the answer to their question the next day. Tuesday was allotted to learning about the different departments and areas of the plant they would be auditing. They began in the morning with the cheese-manufacturing floor. There they saw the beaver again.

"Holy cow," Pep said.

"Holy cow," Rally repeated.

"It's the beaver," they said in unison.

"Yes," their Creature Resources guide said. "This is Eager Beaver, one of our most valued team members. She is the Cheese Machine Maintenance Supervisor."

"Nice to meet you, Eager," Pep said.

"Nice to meet you," Rally said.

"Nice to meet you, Pep and Rally," Eager Beaver said, before the rats could repeat their greeting in unison.

"I thought you were a security guard," Pep blurted out.

"Yeah, we saw you late last night," Rally added.

"Nope, just a regular supervisor," Eager Beaver said. "I was staying late to put together this flow chart for you rats so you would know how things work on the manufacturing floor."

She handed them the charts.

"That wasn't necessary," Pep said.

"You didn't have to work late on our behalf," Rally said.

"They gave us manuals," they chorused.

"I know, but I want things to run as smoothly as possible around here. I thought that a couple of charts would speed up your learning curve," Eager Beaver said.

"Thanks," Pep said.

"Thanks," Rally said.

"Thanks a lot," they said in unison.

The Creature Resources guide looked at her watch.

"Well, it's almost lunchtime. Did you guys hear about the lunch program at The Little Cheese Company?"

"We sure did," Pep said.

"We sure did," Rally repeated.

"It was in the manual," they said in unison.

"Great. Then why don't we meet again after lunch," the Creature Resources guide said. "Thanks for your time, Eager Beaver."

"You are most welcome," Eager Beaver said. "If you rats have any questions, feel free to ask me."

"Thanks," Pep said.

"Thanks," Rally said.

"Are you going to lunch?" they asked the Creature Resources guide in unison.

"Not quite yet," she said. "I have some things I want to get done in my office first."

Pep and Rally had been looking forward to lunch all morning. They rushed to the cafeteria so see what type of food The Little Cheese Company had on offer. When they entered the cafeteria, they stopped in awe. Although the room was nothing special — it was a typical cafeteria with tray lines, stainless steel trim and staff members grouped around tables — but the lunch line was like nothing they had ever seen before. It was piled high with an enormous variety of cheeses of every description and the smells wafting through the room were nothing short of delectable.

"I think I'm in heaven," Pep said.

"It's a rat's dream come true," Rally said.

"Let's eat!" they said in unison.

Other creatures pushed past impatiently, jolting the awe-struck rats out of their reverie. Pep and Rally grabbed plates from the stack and began loading them with free cheese, Pep favoring stinky blue cheeses and Rally going for the milder Jarlsberg, Edam and Swiss varieties. When their plates were so full that the cubes started to tumble off, they sat down and, in between mouthfuls, began reviewing the flow charts Eager Beaver had given them.

As it turned out, Eager Beaver's flow charts were very helpful. The charts allowed them to get a quick overview of operations without having to read all the policies and procedures, product descriptions and general legalese that filled the manuals.

Despite this helpful shortcut, Pep and Rally had so much to learn about The Little Cheese Company that by the end of the first week they were exhausted. The ten-hour days were far longer than they were used to at the car wash so on Friday they vowed to only work an eight-hour day. That way, they would be well rested for Monday.

Week Two

This week, the settling-in period was over and Pep and Rally started their actual work. Now that they knew which departments were to be audited, they began their research looking over documents and familiarizing themselves with processes and past audits. This research took most of the day.

"Whew," Pep said, rubbing his tired eyes.

"Whew," Rally said.

"This is lots of work," they said in unison.

Pep and Rally decided to figure out a way to whittle down their jobs so they wouldn't have to work more than 40 hours a week. They began showing up minutes before 8:00 in the morning and leaving as shortly after 5:00pm as possible. Their goal was to have more time to plan for their own cheese business. Despite their best intentions, however, instead of spending the evening hours planning their cheese-making operation, Pep and Rally spent their free time in front of the television.

"Speaking of needing a break," Pep said, shortly after they arrived at work one morning. "Did you see the break room?"

"No," Rally said.

"I'll show you," Pep said at the exact moment that Rally said, "Show me."

In the hallway, they ran into Eager Beaver.

"Hi, Eager," Pep said.

"Hi, Eager," Rally said.

"Where are you headed?" they said together.

"To the milk processing plant," Eager Beaver said. "I want to make sure we don't have any problems next week when the big milk delivery takes place."

"Really?" Pep said.

"I didn't know you were in the deliveries department," Rally said.

"Oh, I'm not. But it's important that the delivery runs smoothly and I want to help make sure this happens," Eager Beaver said. "How about you guys? I'm sure you're working on the delivery, too."

"Well ..." said Pep.

"Actually ..." said Rally.

"We were going to address that next week," they said in unison.

"On a significant process like milk delivery you may want to ensure everything will run without a hitch ahead of time. Otherwise, you might have to react quickly to keep the milk from spoiling if something goes wrong."

"Yeah," said Pep, shifting his weight from one leg to the other.

"Right," said Rally, trying to hide his reluctance.

They looked at each other.

"Hey, Eager," Rally said, changing the subject. "Did you know there was a break room?"

"Sure, let me show you," Eager Beaver said, leading them down the hall.

"As you can see, The Little Cheese Company provides us with the best gourmet coffee around. The only thing asked for in return is that you contribute a quarter for each cup of coffee you drink."

"Oh, I don't have a quarter," Pep said.

"Me neither," Rally said, padding his pockets.

"We didn't bring quarters," they said in unison, shrugging their shoulders.

"That's okay." Eager Beaver pulled a dollar out of her frock and placed it in the contribution bucket.

Pep and Rally looked at each other. They both had dollars. They didn't think about paying ahead. They felt embarrassed that Eager Beaver had paid for them.

"I'll pay you back tomorrow," Pep said.

"Yeah, I'll pay you back," Rally said.

"We'll pay you back," they said in unison.

Eager Beaver waved them off. "Don't worry about it, guys. Just buy a cup for someone else."

Pep looked at Rally.

Rally looked at Pep.

They both looked at Eager Beaver.

"Why not pay you back?" Pep asked.

"You won't be seeing me here in the break room all that often. It's easier if you just buy someone else a cup of coffee. Plus, it's not a big deal. I'm sure the favor will come back to me."

Seeing the rats' stunned response, Eager Beaver smiled.

"Don't worry about it, guys. Really, it's only a couple of cups of coffee."

"Thanks!" Pep said.

"Thanks!" Rally said.

"Thanks!" they said in unison.

Week Three

As it turned out, Pep and Rally never did get around to buying coffee for anyone else. The next Monday, Pep and Rally took their first coffee break. They wandered to the break room at 10:00am and found Harry, Irene, Jonathan, Kristen and Leslie already there. Pep and Rally remembered their quarters this time but they didn't think to bring enough for anyone else.

When Pep dropped his quarter in the bucket, he noticed that only one other quarter had been put in there since Eager Beaver had contributed her dollar the previous Friday. He pointed to the bucket and looked at Rally but didn't say anything. Rally frowned. Surely someone had enjoyed a cup of super-gourmet coffee since Eager Beaver had paid last week. Rally looked at Harry, Irene, Jonathan, Kristen and Leslie. They were each enjoying a cup of coffee.

Pep looked at Rally.

Rally looked at Pep.

They shrugged in unison.

"This is great coffee," Pep said to the group.

"Great coffee," Rally agreed wholeheartedly.

"Great coffee," they said in unison, taking a seat alongside their workmates.

Harry shrugged.

Irene nodded.

Jonathan looked at his cup as if he hadn't noticed before this moment that he was sipping coffee.

"I suppose," Kristen said.

"It's not that big of a deal," Leslie said with a shrug.

Pep and Rally didn't know what to say. Why wasn't group excited about the coffee?

Now that they had discovered the break room, Pep and Rally made regular visits. They always ran into Harry, Irene, Jonathan, Kristen and Leslie there and they soon got to know each other. Pep looked at the group. "Hey, has anyone seen Eager lately?"

"Yeah, I haven't seen her in a while," Rally said.

No one responded.

"She's always on the manufacturing floor," Harry finally said.

Irene nodded.

"She never takes a break, at least not in here."

"She thinks she's too good for the rest of us," Jonathan said.

Lesley looked at the rats and sneered.

"What's a beaver know about cheese anyway? If you ask me, she should be at the lumber company. That's where she belongs."

Pep and Rally were taken aback by the comments. They liked Eager Beaver. They had no idea others felt this way about her. Just because Eager Beaver worked hard was no reason not to like her. Just because she was a beaver was no reason she shouldn't work in a cheese factory.

Pep and Rally looked around the room, thinking of a way to change the subject.

"Hey," Pep said. "What's that?"

Rally followed Pep's gaze. "Yeah, what *is* that?"

Together they move closer to the bulletin board. "Company picnic," they read in unison.

Harry looked over. "Yeah, the picnic. That's a real fun day."

"Yeah," Irene pitched in. "The Little Cheese Company provides all the cheese and drinks you want."

"But you have to bring crackers or dessert," Jonathan said.

"But it doesn't have to be fancy crackers," Kristen said.

"Last year, I brought wheat crackers that had been sitting in the back of my cupboard for a couple of years," Lesley said proudly.

The others looked at her in surprise, trying to remember if they had eaten any of those crackers with their cheese.

"Does anyone remember that great cheesecake that Eager Beaver brought?" Harry asked.

"That was great cheesecake," Irene said, nodding.

"I had two pieces," Jonathan recalled.

"She made it herself," Kristen said.

"And she still brought crackers – the expensive kind," Leslie added. "Who would spend all that money and time for a company picnic?"

Who would indeed, Pep wondered. It was the same person who wasn't sitting with them in the break room and who overpaid for her coffee. Pep called Rally's attention to another notice on the bulletin board.

"What's this?"

"Big Brothers Big Sisters," they read in unison.

"The Little Cheese Company is always asking us to get involved in charity things," Harry complained.

"They often want us to sign up for some new community thing," Irene said.

"The bosses are always bugging us about getting involved and giving back," Jonathan said. "What are we supposed to give back when we haven't been given anything in the first place?"

Pep thought about the company picnic.

Rally thought about the free lunch.

They both thought about the coffee they hadn't paid for and realized that The Little Cheese Company gives its employees a lot of things that most other companies don't supply their workers.

"I think The Little Cheese Company just wants us out there volunteering so it can get its name in the newspaper," Kristen said.

"Those charities are all scams anyway," Leslie added. "I think they keep the money for themselves."

Pep and Rally looked more closely at the announcement. The bottom half of the posting had a sign-up area. Only Eager Beaver had put her name on the list.

Pep whispered to Rally, "Eager Beaver has signed up."

Harry overheard. "She's always the first on the list," he said.

"Boss's pet," Irene muttered.

"If there were nine more of her, we'd never have to sign up for anything," Jonathan laughed.

"I wish The Little Cheese Company would leave us alone. We're already here from nine to five," Kristen said.

Nine to five? Pep and Rally looked at each other. They had been showing up at 7:45 every morning. They thought working hours were from eight to five – especially since they had an hour lunch break and the meal was free. Now they would be able to sleep in an extra hour in the morning.

"You can just sign up and then not show up. No one will know. And if someone does find out, you can just give them an excuse," Leslie said. "I've never done any of these things. In fact, I might as well sign up for this thing. Who cares if some kid doesn't have anyone to play with on a Saturday afternoon?"

With that, Leslie grabbed a pen and scrawled her name under Eager Beaver's.

Pep considered the posting and thought about all the chores and tasks he needed to do after work and on the weekend. Surely it wasn't fair to sign up to be a Big Brother if he wasn't going to have the time to spend with the kid. Eager Beaver had kids of her own. It wasn't much for her to take on another one or two for the day. But Pep certainly couldn't bring a child to the bar for happy hour on Friday or ask him to watch all the football games he watched on Sundays. He simply didn't have the time.

Rally didn't give the list a second thought. He didn't like children much. Plus, for now he didn't even have time to write a business plan for his own cheese company. Although he could contribute to the blood drive scheduled for next week, he had a fear of needles and the thought of giving blood made him uncomfortable.

Rally shifted his gaze to the floor. There he saw a paper box meant to hold non-perishable items for the food drive. There was one crumpled box of crackers lying in the box. Rally ran a quick mental inventory of his pantry. He had some old pineapple juice he would never drink and a bottle of hot sauce he hadn't opened from a couple of years ago. If he emptied his pantry of all the items that were more than a year old, he could say he'd done his part.

While Rally was thinking about this, he poured himself another cup of coffee. He nodded to himself contentedly before taking a sip. He felt good about donating the food. Hungry homeless people wouldn't care if anything was past its use-by date. They would just be grateful to have something to eat.

Pep and Rally finished their work early on Friday. With more than two hours to kill before 5:00pm they stayed at their computers surfing different websites and pricing out cheese-making equipment. While they were at it, they also placed bids on a few interesting items on eBay they needed to spruce up their homes.

"Hey," Pep said, reading an email from Harry. "Did you hear the one about the three-foot rat?"

"Yeah," Rally replied. "Irene already sent me that joke."

"Funny," they said in unison as they continued perusing their emails and web pages.

Slowly, slowly time passed until it was finally 5:00. When the big hand clicked into the vertical position, Pep shouted, "Hooray!"

"Hooray!" Rally yelled.

Harry, Irene, Jonathan, Kristen and Leslie all yelled "Hooray" and headed out of their offices and towards the front door of The Little Cheese Company. As they scurried down the hallway, they passed Eager Beaver going the other way.

"See you Monday, Eager," Pep said.

"Have a good weekend, Eager," Rally said.

Eager Beaver waved goodbye, barely lifting her eyes from the report she was reading. "Have a great weekend."

"Aren't you leaving?" Pep and Rally asked in unison.

"Soon. I'm still working on the cheese age-tracking process."

"I didn't know you were in the cheese aging department," said Pep.

"I'm not."

"What cheese age-tracking process?" asked Pep blankly.

Beaver looked up. "Oh, I'm sorry. I thought you knew about the trouble we are having keeping track of the cheese-aging process. I'm trying to create a system that streamlines the process and ensures the accuracy of the aging process."

"Wow," Pep and Rally said in unison. They hadn't even heard about the problem, much less felt compelled to work on a solution, especially after 5:00 on a Friday. On Monday they would look into it. Right now, they needed to catch up with the rest of the gang at the Big Rat Saloon for two-for-one happy hour.

There are many benefits to being an employee at The Big Cheese Factory, including complimentary lunch and gourmet coffee during breaks. These benefits are meant to act as a thank you to employees for going above and beyond their regular duties to assist in the growth and development of the company. It is also meant to thank employees who give back to their community by donating their time and money. Many companies have community outreach programs and volunteer programs where employees are encouraged to get involved and contribute.

Many different companies big and small do amazing things for the people who work for and with them. Do you know a company like that? Go to www.MakeYourOwnDamnCheese.com and tell us the story, or read about different companies and their community programs and employee benefits. We hope you can get ideas and take them back to your company and start giving back. Every day, different organizations are looking for volunteers to fill a variety of positions. You yourself can volunteer for an organization you are passionate about, and if you are we want to hear about it!

3

THE BIG CHEESE INCORPORATED BUYOUT

"Did you hear?" Harry asked over the morning cup of coffee.

More than a year had passed since Pep and Rally began working for The Little Cheese Company.

"Hear what?" Pep asked.

"Yeah, hear what?" Rally asked.

After seeing the look on Harry's face, they asked again in unison, "Hear what?"

"The Little Cheese Company is being bought by Big Cheese Incorporated and our jobs are on the chopping block."

Heavy silence descended on the break room group. Fear stabbed each rat's chest.

"What am I going to do?" wailed Irene.

"How am I going to pay my bills?" wondered Jonathan quietly as he sat himself down in a nearby chair to take in the news.

"I don't have any savings," Kristen stammered, her eyes welling with tears.

"I just double-mortgaged my house to buy my new car and pay off my credit card debt," Leslie sobbed.

Pep and Rally took in the news without panic. During their research on cheese before they joined The Little Cheese Company, they had come across a book all about how to embrace change.

"Relax," Pep soothed. "Rally and I are experts on change."

"All you have to do is be ready for change and move with it," Pep added with excitement.

"The important thing is to not be afraid. You will enjoy whatever change happens to offer you," Rally said smugly.

"Change with change and enjoy the new opportunities," Pep concluded.

Harry, Irene, Jonathan, Kristen and Leslie stared at Pep and Rally like they were crazy. What new opportunities? All they could see looming in the future was financial strife.

"Well, I better get to work," Harry said.

"Me too," Irene said.

They left the break room and were closely followed by Jonathan and Kristen. Leslie continued drinking her coffee, all the while wondering whether she had enough equity in her house to sell it, the advantages of bankruptcy and how long her unemployment checks would last. Pep and Rally looked at each other and the stack of used coffee cups piled in the sink and crowded on the counter. They shrugged.

"I guess no one else has ever read a book about change," Pep said.

"Evidently not," Rally said.

"Well, we better get to work ourselves." Pep stuck his cup inside another one, splashing some coffee on the counter.

"Yeah, we better get ready for change," Rally said, sliding his coffee cup across the counter towards the sink.

But things didn't quite turn out as Pep and Rally had planned.

"What?" shrieked Pep.

"No way!" said Rally.

"That's impossible!" they shouted together.

Pep and Rally stood in their office. Official looking envelopes had just been delivered to them. Thinking they were notices of corporate change, they opened their envelopes in excitement. Instead, the envelopes contained pink slips.

"This is bad," said Pep.

"Really bad," said Rally.

"This is really, really bad," they said together.

You see, Pep and Rally were sure there would be change. They just hadn't planned on this type of change. Instead of planning for various types for change and considering different potential circumstances, they had been organizing their offices and files. They were certain Big Cheese Incorporated would give them new procedures for auditing its departments. They were sure they would be given new responsibilities and answer to new bosses. They were positive that they would be given new offices or possibly moved to Big Cheese Incorporated's main office. They had even looked on the Internet for living quarters near Big Cheese Incorporated's headquarters.

What they hadn't anticipated was being downsized, right sized, outsized or resized. They were sure the folks at Big Cheese Incorporated would realize their knowledge of cheeses. After all, they had probably sampled more cheeses than anyone else who worked at The Little Cheese Company, and many of them were made by Big Cheese Incorporated.

Pep and Rally understood why Big Cheese Incorporated would let Harry, Irene, Jonathan, Kristen and Leslie go – they were clearly not good team members. But Pep and Rally could not believe they were lumped with the rest of the rats. They may have become a bit complacent and comfortable in their jobs but they were far from lazy, they told themselves. And who, apart from Eager Beaver, didn't do the minimum their jobs required? They did what they were being paid for and didn't owe anyone more than that, did they? Sure, they watched the clock and looked forward to breaks, lunches and quitting time, but who didn't? When asked to help out in other departments or contribute to tasks that lay outside their job descriptions, Pep and Rally knew they hemmed and hawed and tried to get out of it and they had become good at looking busy when bosses passed by. Although Pep and Rally didn't see the point of exerting themselves unnecessarily, for the most part they felt they did a good job and were securely employed.

"What are we going to do?" wailed Pep.

"What are we going to do?" wailed Rally.

"We're doomed!" they wailed together.

In a daze, they wandered to the break room. Harry, Irene, Jonathan, Kristen and Leslie were already there looking pale and whispering to each other.

"You guys too?" asked Harry.

Pep and Rally nodded.

"They fired all of us," Jonathan said.

"And with only two weeks' severance," Kristen whined.

Leslie just shook her head in disbelief.

"But they can't fire me," Harry declared. "I have seniority. I have worked here for 20 years."

"I'm pregnant. They can't fire me when I'm pregnant. I'll sue them," Irene screeched.

The others looked at Irene in surprise.

"Well, I will be," Irene said defensively. "That way they can't fire me. They won't know when I actually got pregnant."

"I'm a veteran," Jonathan added, slamming his fist on the table.

"I have a degree from Harvard," Kristen declared angrily.

"I'm red," Leslie said. "I'll sue them for fur color discrimination."

Pep looked at Rally. Rally looked at Pep. Although they thought their knowledge of cheese would have protected them from the downsizing, they weren't about to bring it up.

"I heard Eager Beaver didn't get fired," Harry sneered.

"I hear she's moving to Big Cheese Incorporated's headquarters," Irene scoffed.

"Apparently, she got a management position," Jonathan said.

"With a pay raise," added Kristen.

"I'm sure we can all guess how a beaver got a promotion in a cheese company," Leslie snickered.

The group looked gloomily into their coffee cups, trying to come to terms with their situation.

"At least we'll get unemployment benefits after the severance ends," Harry thought out loud.

"By then we will be able to get new jobs somewhere else," Irene said.

"That should be plenty of time," Jonathan said.

"It's not fair that a beaver should get promoted over us," Kristen said. "What makes her so qualified for a management position?"

"A rat should have her job," scowled Leslie.

No one in the break room could understand why Eager Beaver had been promoted when the rest of them were facing such an uncertain future.

"It's not fair," grumbled Pep.

"It's not fair," mumbled Rally.

"It's not fair!" the group cried in unison.

4

SAMPLING THE BREAD OF SHAME

Things for Pep and Rally only worsened. After their two weeks' severance ended, they still hadn't found any work. And it wasn't like they weren't trying. They visited every cheese factory in town. They even applied to be servers at the cheeseburger restaurant. They knew things were really bad when they applied to process soybeans at the vegetarian cheese factory. Few jobs were available, and those that were had hundreds of applicants. There weren't even any job openings at the old car wash where they used to work.

When their severance ran out, Pep had to let his apartment go and move in with Rally. Rally sold his car and shared Pep's. They could no longer afford cheese, so they began to eat bread to save money. They signed up for unemployment benefits and joined the government bread program.

Pep and Rally missed eating cheese. They almost wept when they had to eat government bread without cheese on it. The more they thought about how hungry they were, the hungrier they became. The more they concentrated on how they didn't have cheese to eat, the worse they felt about not having cheese. The more they dwelt on the desperation of their situation, the more desperate it grew. They became so depressed they couldn't budge off their couch.

Things were worse the next week.

They worsened the week after that.

The week after that was worse than all the previous weeks combined.

Could the week after that get any worse?

"We have to do something," Pep said.

"We have to do something," Rally agreed.

"We have to do something soon," they said in unison.

They sat in their living room together, staring at a platter of bread. Neither one of them could break off another bite. How much longer would they have to eat bread? This was shameful.

"Maybe we should see if Eager Beaver can help us out," Pep said.

"She has lots of money," Rally said. "I'm sure she can help."

"We should call her," they said in unison.

"She's probably at work," Pep said.

"It's only 3:30," Rally said.

"She's probably at work," they said in unison.

It was winter, so the days were shorter and night came early. Because they had to save money, Pep and Rally didn't turn the lights on while watching television. Fortunately, the TV was large enough to light the entire room as well as the adjoining bathroom. As long as the TV was on, there was no need to turn on a lamp.

Pep noticed how the television light illuminated the platter of half-eaten bread sitting on the coffee table in front of them.

"This is such a shame," Pep said.

"Such a shame," Rally agreed.

"A real shame," they said in unison.

"What time is it?" Pep asked.

Rally hit the information button on the remote. "6:36."

"We should call Eager," they said in unison.

The phone bill hadn't been paid in months and the phone company had finally resorted to cutting the line so Pep and Rally had to walk to the payphone at the corner of their street. They didn't have a quarter, so they called collect. They needed to save money anyway. Plus, Eager Beaver made enough of it to afford a collect call.

"Hi, Eager," Pep said, after Eager Beaver accepted the charges.

"Hi, Pep. It is so good to hear from you. How have you been?"

"Oh, not so good."

"I am sorry to hear that — very, very sorry. Have you heard from Rally?"

"Yes, he is right here with me."

"How is he doing?"

"About the same as me. We're roommates now."

"That's great," Eager Beaver said encouragingly. "It's good to live with friends."

"Well, we kind of have to share a place."

Eager Beaver didn't say anything.

Pep looked at Rally. "Um, that's sort of why I'm calling. You see, Rally and I haven't been able to find work."

"I'm sorry to hear that."

"Yeah, and well, we were wondering if there was any way you could help us out. Maybe loan us some cheese or something."

Eager Beaver didn't say anything.

Pep looked at Rally.

"Wouldn't you guys rather pursue your true potential?" Eager Beaver asked.

"Well, yes, but in the meantime we are really tired of eating bread."

"The Bread of Shame," Eager Beaver said knowingly.

"Huh?" asked Pep.

"The Bread of Shame," Eager Beaver repeated.

"Um, yes it is a shame. That's why we would like to borrow some cheese," Pep said, returning to his positive pitch.

"No, you don't understand me. The two of you have been eating the Bread of Shame. If I simply hand you some cheese, I will be contributing to your Bread of Shame."

"Oh, we don't need any more bread," Pep answered. "The government gives us plenty of bread. We just want something to go with the bread. Even peanut butter would be fine right about now."

"You're not understanding me," Eager Beaver said in an authoritative voice, trying to get Pep's attention. She paused, thought for a moment, and continued. "I'll tell you what, tomorrow is Saturday. Why don't I take you and Rally on a picnic."

"No that's okay. If you could just drop off some cheese at our apartment, that would be fine."

"You don't want to go on a picnic?" Eager Beaver asked.

"Well, the college football games are on tomorrow and if we go to Freddy's bar, they have dollar beers and free chips. We can eat the chips all afternoon and only buy one beer."

Eager Beaver was silent for a moment.

"I guess I won't be able to help you then. I'm sorry you can't join me for a picnic. I hope to hear from you again soon, Pep."

With that, Eager Beaver hung up the phone.

"What'd she say?" asked Rally.

"She invited us on a picnic."

"A what?" Rally asked in shock.

"A picnic," Pep said incredulously.

"Why?"

"I don't know," Pep shrugged, looking confused.

"What'd you say?"

"I said it was dollar-beer day, of course," Pep said.

"Plus, it's too cold for a picnic," Rally said.

"Too cold for a picnic," they said in unison.

Things took a turn for the worse the following week.

On Saturday, the bartender kicked Pep and Rally out of the bar at 2:00pm after only a couple of handfuls of chips.

On Sunday, they were banned from watching NFL games at another bar offering free chips and peanuts. The bakery didn't have any more free samples for them on Monday.

On Tuesday, they were barred from the wholesale store because they ate too many samples from there too.

On Wednesday, the all-you-can eat buffet kicked them out after four hours.

They tried to leave a restaurant without paying for lunch on Thursday but without a car, it was easy for the server to chase after them.

They gave up on Friday.

"We should call Eager," Pep said

"We should definitely call Eager," Rally said.

"Let's call Eager," they said in unison.

At 6:30 that evening, Pep and Rally were back at the pay phone. This time Rally dialed Eager Beaver's number.

"Hi, Eager, it's Rally."

"Rally, I'm so glad you called. After talking to Pep last week I have been worrying about you two rats."

"Oh, um, thanks."

"How is Pep?" Eager Beaver asked.

"Oh, um, the same."

"That's too bad. Are you guys still eating the Bread of Shame?"

"Um, just government bread and whatever else we can scrape up," Rally replied.

"That's too bad."

"Well, actually, we were wondering if you still wanted to go on a picnic," Rally asked in a soft voice.

"Of course, I would love to spend time with you guys. But what about dollar-beer day?"

"Well, that isn't working out so well," Rally admitted.

"Really?"

"Yeah, we're free tomorrow if you are."

"Certainly. I would love to spend some time with you fellows. Let me just check my schedule."

Eager Beaver paused and came back to the phone.

"I am volunteering tomorrow at the children's hospital. I'm going with my kids to read stories to children on the cancer ward. But I'm free on Sunday."

"Sunday is fine," Rally said quickly.

"Great, I'll be by your apartment at nine."

"Nine in the morning or evening?" Rally asked.

Eager Beaver laughed. "Nine in the evening is a little late for a picnic, especially since we all have to be up early Monday morning."

Rally had been thinking the opposite. Nine in the morning was a little early for a picnic, especially since he and Pep rarely got out of bed before ten.

"Nine in the morning seems early for a picnic," he said.

"We have a bit of a long drive ahead of us," said Eager.

"I suppose we can be up by then."

"Great. I'll see you at 9:00." Eager Beaver hung up the phone.

"What'd she say?" asked Pep.

"She's going to pick us up at 9:00 on Sunday," Rally answered.

"In the morning or evening?" asked Pep.

"Morning."

"But I won't be up yet," Pep whined.

"She said we have a ways to drive."

"Where are we going?"

"I don't know," Rally admitted.

"That's a lot of trouble for a picnic. Can't we just go to a local park?" Pep asked.

Rally thought of something. "Hey, did she say something last time about the Shame Bread?"

"Yeah, she said it was a shame we were eating bread."

"No, she said it differently, like it was called Shame Bread."

"Yeah," Pep said. "Actually, she did say it like that."

"What do you think that means?"

"I have no idea."

"Me neither," Rally said. "Maybe we should go to the grocery store and find this Shame Bread. Maybe it's cheaper."

"Could be," Pep said.

"Shame Bread?" they wondered in unison.

5

FIELD TRIP TO
THE FOREST OF HIDDEN POTENTIAL

Eager Beaver arrived at Pep and Rally's apartment at 8:53 on Sunday morning. Neither Pep nor Rally was awake. It had been so long since they had to set the alarm clock that they had set it to go off at 8:30pm instead of 8:30am.

Eager Beaver knocked on the door.

"Who's that?" asked Pep wearily.

"Who's that?" asked Rally, rubbing his eyes.

"It's Eager," they said in unison. They shot up from bed and rushed around each other throwing on their blue overalls before answering the door.

"Hello, Eager," huffed Pep.

"Hello, Eager," said Rally, out of breath.

"Hello, you guys," Eager Beaver replied cheerfully.

The apartment was so cluttered and disorganized that Pep and Rally were too embarrassed to invite Eager Beaver inside. Plates filled with breadcrumbs were stacked in the sink. Socks and shoes were scattered throughout the living room and a platter of bread was still on the living room coffee table. Magazines they had 'borrowed' from various waiting rooms were strewn all over the floor and the plant in the corner had died weeks ago.

"Hold on a second," Pep said.

"I'll just get my coat," Rally said.

"We'll be right back," they said in unison.

Eager Beaver waited patiently in her car for Pep and Rally as they frantically rushed to get themselves ready for the picnic. It wasn't quite as cold outside as they had feared it would be, but they still wanted to dress warmly, just in case. Pep had misplaced his favorite cap. It was the one his ears fit through perfectly. And Rally couldn't track down his striped coat. Pep and Rally fervently tore apart their apartment looking for the missing garments. The clutter worsened as they became more frantic.

"I found it!" shouted Pep, putting on his cap.

"I found it!" shouted Rally, waving his coat in the air.

"Let's go!" they shouted in unison.

Pep and Rally tumbled into Eager Beaver's car.

"Nice car," Pep said snidely. Eager Beaver was driving the same minivan she was driving when they worked together at The Little Cheese Company.

"Thank you," Eager Beaver replied, oblivious to the sarcasm.

"I thought you would have bought a more modern, fancy car with your new job." Rally said.

"No, this one works just fine."

"But you should be making better money now," Pep prompted.

"I am, but my lifestyle hasn't changed much. We live on almost the same amount of money each month and invest the rest for the children's educations, my retirement and, of course, charity."

"It's easier to save and give to charity when you have more money," Rally said.

"Actually, I contributed to savings and charity when I worked at The Little Cheese Company, too."

"Oh," said Pep.

"Oh," said Rally.

"Hmmm," they said in unison, realizing they had actually made more money than Eager Beaver at The Little Cheese Company.

Pep tried to change the subject. "So, where are we headed?"

"Have you ever heard of the Forest of Hidden Potential?" Eager Beaver asked.

Anxiety tugged at Pep's chest. "Isn't that the place with the sign that says 'Dare not Enter'?" he asked.

Eager Beaver laughed. "That's funny, Pep."

"Well, doesn't it?" asked Rally. "I've seen the sign myself."

"Rats, the sign says D.A.R.E."

"Right," said Pep.

"Right," said Rally.

"That's what we said," they said in unison.

"No rats, it says D.A.R.E. It's an acronym. D stands for Dream. A stands for Act on your dream. R is for Realize your true potential, and E means be Excited about life."

"How'd you know that?" Pep asked.

"Yeah, who told you?" Rally asked.

Eager Beaver waited for more questions, but none came. "I've visited the Forest of Hidden Potential many times. My friend Richard taught me its meaning."

Eager Beaver slowed the car. "Hey, would you guys like to have some coffee?"

"Oh yes, I'd love some coffee," Pep said.

"Me too," Rally said.

"We haven't had coffee since it was available for free at The Little Cheese Company," they said in unison.

"It was never *free*," Eager Beaver reminded them as her eyes widened. "You paid a quarter for each cup you drank. Didn't you?"

"Uh," said Pep, not knowing how to answer.

"Yeah," said Rally unconvincingly.

"Usually," they said in unison.

Pep and Rally looked at each other in shame.

"Um, sometimes we forgot," Pep admitted.

"Yeah, sometimes we forgot," Rally said.

They both turned red with embarrassment.

When they stopped at a café and each had a steaming cup of coffee in front of them, Pep drummed up some courage to ask Eager a question.

"Eager, I've been wanting to ask you, when Big Cheese Incorporated bought The Little Cheese Company, why were we all downsized while you got a promotion?"

"Do you really want to know?" Eager Beaver asked.

"Yes," said Pep, nodding his head.

"Yes," said Rally, doing the same.

"Please tell us," they begged in unison.

"Before I do tell you, let me ask *you* a question: Why did you decide you wanted to work for The Little Cheese Company in the first place?"

"To make money, of course" Pep said.

"Actually, that's not why," Rally reminded him. "We wanted to work there to learn about the cheese business."

"And why did you want to learn about the cheese business?" asked Eager Beaver.

"Because we wanted to make our own cheese," Pep said. He hadn't thought about making cheese in over a year.

"Really?" Eager Beaver asked.

"Yeah, we wanted to make our own special kind of cheese," Rally admitted.

"Really?" Eager Beaver asked again.

"Yes," Pep and Rally said in unison.

"So why haven't you gotten off your duffs to make your own @#$! cheese?" she asked with a sudden and very loud smack of her tail.

Eager Beaver's fury and the tremendous clap of her tail shocked Pep and Rally. Not only had they never heard her say "*@#$!*" before, but she was rarely so direct and passionate when she questioned others. She definitely did have a point though. Why *hadn't* they gotten off their duffs to make their own @#$! cheese? It seemed like being downsized would have been the perfect opportunity for the rats to shift their focus back to their original plan, but ...

Before they could come up with a response, Eager Beaver continued.

"We all have the opportunity to get off our duffs to make our own @#$! cheese *each and every single day.* Every day we have the opportunity to reach our full and true potential."

Pep and Rally stared at her, waiting for her to go on.

"But you got too comfortable," Eager Beaver continued, "and that distracted you from your full potential. Your workday began later every day. Your lunch breaks stretched to an hour and half and you ran out the door right at 5:00. You wasted so much time in your day that you never actually got any work done. Instead of getting off your duffs and concentrating on learning how to make your own @#$! cheese, you watched the clock."

"But how were we supposed to make our own cheese while working for The Little Cheese Company?" Pep asked defensively.

"We were only auditors," Rally added.

"What were we supposed to do?" they asked in unison.

"Well, let me ask again. Why did you want to work at The Little Cheese Company?"

"To learn the cheese business," Pep repeated.

"So why didn't you get off your duffs and apply yourselves to learning the cheese business?   You were auditing different departments. You could have taken an extra moment to learn more about these departments and how they functioned. You could have gone beyond what you covered in your audits. You could have spent time meeting the various team members in each department and asked them questions about the cheese business. Instead, you became too comfortable and failed to reach your full potential. Then, to top it all off, you reduced yourselves to having to feast on the Bread of Shame."

"You mentioned the Shame Bread before," said Pep.

"Yeah, you said it before," Rally agreed.

"We looked for Shame Bread in the store," Pep said. "We thought it might be cheaper."

"It wasn't there," Rally added.

"What is Shame Bread?" they asked in unison.

Eager Beaver laughed. "The Bread of Shame isn't a brand of bread, it is a metaphor for taking something without giving back or receiving something you don't truly deserve. Did you rats enjoy the free cheese the company offered its employees during lunch?"

"Yes!" cheered Pep, recalling his favorite cheese varieties.

"That was the best part of working for The Little Cheese Company," Rally added, his whiskers twitching just thinking about all that cheese.

"Free cheese!" they said in unison.

"What did you do to deserve the free cheese?" Eager Beaver asked.

"We worked," Pep said.

"Yeah, we worked," Rally said.

"We deserved the cheese," they said in unison.

"Actually, you *didn't* deserve the cheese. You were being paid wages to do your job. The free cheese was a bonus. The company didn't have to give it to you. If you had actually worked extra hard or extended hours, then you might have deserved a token of appreciation from the company. Instead, you happily took the cheese but didn't do anything out of the ordinary to truly deserve it. This added to your shame."

"You didn't eat the free cheese?" Pep asked.

"Yeah, didn't you take lunch?" Rally asked.

"Hey, we saw you in the cafeteria," they said in unison.

"You are right, but I didn't sit in the cafeteria while I ate. Instead, I ate on the manufacturing floor. I spent time reading about cheese manufacturing, machine maintenance and other areas to help The Little Cheese Company succeed. I showed my appreciation for the free cheese by returning the favor. It's what I call giving back."

"Oh," Pep said sheepishly.

"I didn't know that," Rally said.

"Oh," they said in unison.

Eager Beaver continued. "When the company asked you to do extra work or to volunteer for its charities, did you ever sign up?"

"I didn't have the time," replied Pep.

"I didn't have the money," responded Rally.

"We didn't have enough time or money," they said in unison.

"Really?" Eager Beaver questioned. "It would have been a glorious way to show your appreciation for the free cheese, the company picnic, even the delicious gourmet coffee in the break room."

Pep hung his head.

Rally squirmed uncomfortably.

Their whiskers drooped.

"Even something as simple as taking samples from the grocery store without any intention to buy something adds to the Bread of Shame," Eager Beaver said.

"Oh," Pep said.

"Oh," Rally said.

"We've been doing that pretty much every day," they admitted in unison.

"I know. And that is why this lay off has been so difficult for you two rats. The more Bread of Shame that you think you must eat, the harder it becomes for you to live up to your potential. That's why I couldn't just give you the cheese when you asked for it."

"Why not?" Pep asked.

"Why not?" Rally asked.

"Yeah, why not?" they asked in unison.

"Because then I would be adding to your Bread of Shame. I would be giving you something you didn't deserve or earn. I would be making it worse for you if I helped you the way you wanted me to help you. Sure, you might have had some cheese for a day or two but then you wouldn't have changed your situation. Instead of getting off your duffs and making your own @#$! cheese, like you know you should be, you would keep coming back to me or going to someone else for more free cheese!"

"Then why are you taking us on a picnic?" Pep asked, somewhat confused.

"Yeah, why are you taking us on a picnic?" Rally asked.

"Why?" they asked in unison.

"For the record, I'm not taking you on just any picnic. I am taking you on a picnic at the Forest of Hidden Potential. Here you will learn to get off your duff and reach your fullest potential instead of adding to your Bread of Shame."

"But you're still giving us something," Pep said.

"Yeah, you're still giving us lunch, right?" Rally said worriedly.

"You're still giving stuff to us," they said in unison.

"No, I'm allowing you an opportunity to reach your full potential. You will each have to decide for yourselves whether or not to continue eating the Bread of Shame."

Eager Beaver nodded at the sign they were approaching. "Here we are," she said cheerfully.

6

DARE-ING TO ENTER
THE FOREST OF HIDDEN POTENTIAL

The sign was really a big rock with the letters D.A.R.E carved into its surface.

"We've never known anyone who has been past the sign," Pep said dubiously.

"I've heard it's dangerous," Rally said.

"Scary and dangerous," they said in unison.

"Who told you it was dangerous?" Eager Beaver asked.

"Everyone," Pep said.

"*All* the rats say it is," said Rally.

"*Everyone*," they said in unison.

"They don't understand the sign then they don't know the true meaning of D.A.R.E. If they did understand, they would not be so fearful. Their fears are based on an assumption of what they see," Eager Beaver said.

As they drove on past the sign, she began to explain its meaning.

"The sign at the edge of this forest is telling you to: **Dream** your dreams. You do this by being creative and inventing ways to reach your full potential. Next, you need to **Act** upon your dreams. Acting requires you to **Realize** your true potential to achieve your dreams. Then what you need is some real **Excitement** for life. This involves knowing that you are the sole cause and reason for your own success. In other words, you are in control of your life. It's that simple."

"D.A.R.E," Pep said.

"D.A.R.E," Rally repeated.

"Dream, Act, Realize and be Excited," they recited in unison.

"You've got it right this time. Let's have some cheese before we walk through the Forest of Hidden Potential," suggested Eager Beaver, plopping herself on the ground.

"Hooray!" cheered Pep.

"Hooray!" cheered Rally.

"Cheese!" they cheered in unison.

Eager Beaver shook her head in dismay. They still had so much to learn.

The cheese was wonderful. Eager Beaver had purchased the best cheeses from the Big Cheese Incorporated store. To the two hungry rats, cheese had never tasted so good. They mixed cow's milk cheese with goat's milk cheese, and hard cheeses with sheep's milk cheeses, and on and on until they couldn't eat any more.

"Thank you, Eager," Pep said, patting his belly.

"Thank you, Eager" Rally said, patting his belly too.

"Thank you so much," they said in unison as they patted their bellies.

"Now you guys have to walk off all that cheese. Are you ready to enter the Forest of Hidden Potential?" Eager Beaver said as she stood up.

Pep and Rally had enjoyed the cheese so much they had all but forgotten their fear of the forest. "Let's go," they said in unison.

The threesome walked together along a mossy path. Pep and Rally found out quickly that the Forest of Hidden Potential wasn't as scary or dangerous as everyone said. In fact, it was beautiful. Trees stood tall. Birds were chirping. Sunlight filtered through the treetops and the scent of the forest was fresh and crisp. It was truly a magnificent forest. Pep and Rally began to wonder if the others had told them the scary stories of danger to keep them out of the Forest of Hidden Potential.

After sniffing and scurrying about for ten minutes, Pep saw something that caught his attention.

"Check this out," he said.

"What is that?" Rally asked, looking up.

"It looks like a face in the tree," they said in unison.

"Yes, it is," Eager Beaver said. "Many of the trees have faces. This is Warren Buffet's face. Buffet is a man who continues to reach his full potential today. His first job was writing stock prices on a chalkboard at his father's brokerage firm. When he was 13, he delivered newspapers for $175 a month. He filed income tax that year, deducting his bicycle as a business expense. When he was 14 he took the $1,200 he had saved and purchased 40 acres of farmland. He then rented his land to a farmer."

"Wow, he started young," Pep interjected.

"In high school," Eager Beaver continued, "Buffet and a couple of friends purchased a pinball machine for $25 and put it in a barber shop. Buffet later purchased three other machines and put them in various locations. A year later he sold the business for $1,200.

"From those beginnings Buffet eventually became the second wealthiest man in the world. But Buffet didn't horde his wealth. He donated 85 per cent of his fortune to the Bill and Melinda Gates Foundation. This nearly $31 billion is the largest charitable donation in history."

"Amazing," Pep said.

"Really amazing," Rally said.

"Look over there," Pep pointed.

"Hey, look," Rally said.

"It's Oprah Winfrey," they said in unison."Yes," Eager Beaver said. "Oprah has a very recognizable face. And she's one amazing woman. She came from impoverished beginnings to become one of the wealthiest women in the world. But one gets the sense that Oprah is less concerned

Warren Buffett

with money and more interested in achieving her full potential which for her means being a role model and messenger to millions of people.

"Born to poor, unmarried teenagers, Oprah Winfrey was raised by her grandmother who taught her to read at three years old. When she was 17, Oprah worked at a local radio station. Later, she became the youngest news anchor of her time. She was then recruited to host a morning talk show in Chicago. Within months of debuting, Oprah took the show from last place rating to first place. This was the show that would become *The Oprah Winfrey Show*. But Oprah has been active in many areas beyond her show — acting, producing and even magazine publishing. She also gives significant amounts of her time and money to help others in need both in the United States and beyond.

"Do you recognize that person?" Eager Beaver asked, shifting her gaze to a different tree.

"Yeah," Pep said, somewhat unsure.

"Hmm," Rally said, not sure who it was either.

"That's Steve Jobs," Eager Beaver said.

"Oh yeah," Pep and Rally said in unison.

"He co-founded Apple computers and was also CEO of Pixar. When he was

Oprah

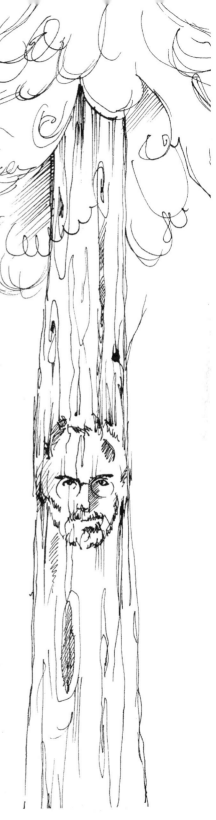

pushed out of Apple in 1985, he didn't give up. Instead, he developed a new computer company called NeXT. Eleven years later, Apple bought this company to boost its technological standing and Jobs returned to Apple. Under his direction, the company expanded into portable music players. Now everyone has an iPod or some other MP3 player. And the iPhone, which came next, has changed how people think about their telephone.

Eager Beaver pointed at another tree. "Over there is George Washington Carver. He was born into slavery. But that didn't stop him. He did a lot of good things for American farmers. He is best known for inventing 300 different uses for the peanut—peanut butter was not one of them."

"Oh," Pep said.

Then Rally asked, "Who's that old guy on the motorcycle?"

"That's David Oreck. At his age he still drives his motorcycles to work. He also flies biplanes for fun.

"Shortly after World War II, Oreck began working for RCA. During that time, the company's Whirlpool division was having difficulty selling its upright vacuum cleaners. Oreck analyzed this failure and discovered he could redesign the vacuums and turn them into a

Steve Jobs

successful product. Whirlpool agreed to give Oreck exclusive rights to redesign and sell the vacuums.

"In 1963 he started his own company, Oreck Corporation. Originally, Oreck Corp built upright vacuum cleaners for hotel use. When the housekeeping staff asked to buy the vacuums for their homes, Oreck decided to make vacuums for the general consumer and made a fortune."

As they walked, Eager Beaver pointed out another tree. "Have you fellows ever bought anything on eBay?"

"Yeah, at work," Pep said enthusiastically without a second thought. "I outbid someone on a great cheese knife."

Eager Beaver slapped her tail.

Pep hung his head remembering how often he too would surf the Internet at work, looking up things that had nothing to do with his job.

"Anyway," Eager Beaver continued curtly, bringing their attention back to the face on the closest tree, "Meg Whitman started working with eBay when the company only had thirty employees. She already had a successful career working for large companies but she signed on with

Meg Whitman

eBay and managed to turn it into a household name. From 1998 up until March 2008 she was the president and CEO of eBay. Today she continues as a member of the board."

Pep looked around and found another recognizable face. He pointed at it and said, "But wait."

Rally saw what Pep was pointing at. "There's more," said Pep.

"Set it and forget it," they said in unison.

"That's right," Eager Beaver laughed. "That's Ron Popeil."

"Back when I could afford cheese and had a job, I would often 'set it and forget it'," Pep said.

"I still have one of those chopping things under my sink," Rally said.

"He has definitely made people's lives easier with his inventions," Eager Beaver said. "Back in 1951, when he was 16 years old, Popeil's job was to demonstrate his father's inventions at different stores. When storeowners and managers saw how easy it was to sell the inventions, they would buy Popeil senior's inventions. From that early success, Popeil realized he could sell his own inventions directly to people rather than through department stores like Sears and JC Penny's. "With the advent of television, Popeil adapted what he had learned from selling on city streets and fairs to the new medium. Soon, all of America knew about the Chop-O-Matic, Veg-O-

Summer Redstone

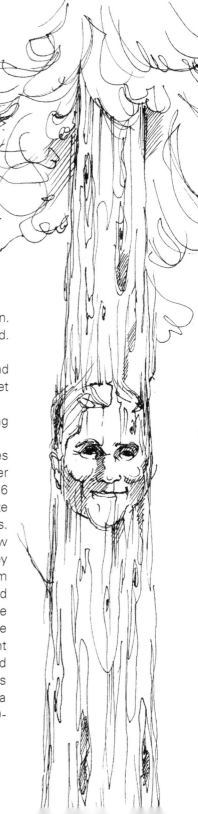

Matic and the Pocket Fisherman. Soon he was making $1,000 a week at a time when most people made $500 a month."

"Speaking of television," Eager Beaver added, "Do you know who this is?"

"No," the rats said in unison.

"This is Sumner Redstone. He started off with a promising career as an attorney but it was in his leadership of Viacom and CBS that he reached his full potential.

"In World War II he was a code breaker for the army. After the war, Redstone graduated with a law degree from Harvard Law School. He actively pursued that line of work while also helping his father develop the family business—a theater chain.

"Under Redstone's direction, the National Amusements theater chain went through a successful expansion. Through his involvement with the theaters, Redstone learned a lot about the movie industry. Believing that content would become more important than distribution chains, Redstone began investing in movie studios. He would eventually sell these investments and purchase Viacom. With this company, he focused on syndicating television shows that other companies produced. This success led to his purchase of cable channels. Redstone made Viacom a major media empire."

"So everyone here is an entrepreneur?" Rally asked.

"No, they have just reached their full potential. We happen to be aware of the **Jan Lafferty** successful entrepreneurs but there are many more people reaching their full potential every day in ways we don't see. Let me show you one of my personal favorites."

Eager Beaver led the rats to a particularly tall tree.

"Wow," Pep said.

"She's beautiful," Rally said.

"Wow," they said in unison.

"This lady is a personal role model of mine," Eager Beaver said.

"Have you ever been to Las Vegas?" she asked Pep and Rally.

"No," they said in unison. "But we've seen it on television."

"Jan Laverty Jones is one lady who definitely reached her full potential. Not content to let society define what she should do, she became the first woman mayor of Las Vegas in 1991. That might not seem like a big deal, but Las Vegas is an old-boy's club, kind of like Big Cheese Incorporated is a rat's club. But Jones became so popular she won a second term as mayor. From there she became an executive with Harrah's Entertainment, another traditionally old-boy's industry—the casino business.

"But Jones didn't just pursue her own career; she also supported those around her. When Harrah's wanted to cut her department to save money, the company wanted to keep her and move her to another position, but Jones stood up for others. She told Harrah's executives to cut her and keep the other employees. They saw how valuable she was and not only kept her, but also kept her department."

Jenna Bush

"Look," said Pep. Jenna Bush is here too.

"Didn't she write a book recently?" asked Rally.

"Yes," added Eager Beaver. "It's called *Ana's Story: A Journey of Hope*. It's about a 17-year-old single mother in Panama who is living with HIV. Bush wanted to write about the things she saw while working for UNICEF. She's hoping the book will inspire kids to help make a difference in the world."

Eager Beaver continued on to someone else. "Check out this person."

"Who's that?" Pep and Rally asked.

"This is Sheldon Adelson," Eager Beaver said. "He's the third wealthiest man in the world. In fact, he moved from the fourteenth wealthiest to third in only three years. He makes more than one million dollars an hour."

"Wow," Pep said.

"How'd he do that?" Rally asked.

"He started out as a poor child selling newspapers on the street corner in Boston. He eventually created and built 50 companies. He bought the Sands Hotel and Casino in 1989. He tore it down to make way for The Venetian Hotel and Casino — one of the most beautiful casinos in the world. Adelson also built the Sands Macao in China. And soon you will see another casino in Singapore."

"We should visit it one day," Pep said.

"Here is someone who should be important to the two of you," Eager Beaver said, leading the rats to a tree where the face of a friendly familiar man smiled down at them.

"Holy cow," Pep said.

"Holy cow," Rally said.

Sheldon Adelson

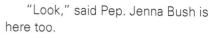

"That's weird," they said in unison.

"That's right," Eager Beaver said. "That's Spencer Johnson. He wrote an important book about cheese and change. Even though he had a successful medical career, his true potential was reached through helping people and companies deal with change. Now tens of millions of people around the world have benefited from reading his book."

Pep and Rally looked at each other.

"And over here is Robert Kiyosaki," Eager Beaver pointed out. "You've read one of his books, haven't you?"

Pep and Rally looked at each other. In fact, they had read the book about rich dads back when they were thinking of making their own cheese. They were both thinking they should read the book again and begin applying its lessons to their own lives.

While he recounted the principles Kiyosaki taught, Pep's attention moved to another thought provoking face on a tree. "Look, a guy on a bicycle."

"That's Lance Armstrong," Eager Beaver said. "He not only won more Tour de France bicycle races than anyone else, he set this record between 1999 and 2005. This happened after surgery and chemotherapy for testicular cancer that had metastasized to his brain and lungs in 1996. He went from having a less than 40 per cent chance of survival to seven consecutive victories at the Tour de

Spencer Johnson

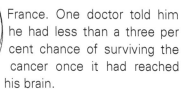

France. One doctor told him he had less than a three per cent chance of surviving the cancer once it had reached his brain.

"In 1997 he launched the Lance Armstrong Foundation to support cancer victims. The foundation has raised tens of millions of dollars, thanks in part to the yellow wristbands the foundation distributes.

"You see, not everyone reaches their true potential through their work. In fact, most of us reach our full potential in our everyday lives. These trees are full of mothers and fathers, neighbors and just plain nice people. We don't necessarily recognize them because they are not famous personalities who often appear in the newspaper. But potentially, they do more than even the most successful business people and athletes."

"So you don't have to be a celebrity?" Rally asked.

"No, you just have to reach your full potential every day of your life," Eager Beaver replied. "For instance, look at that tree."

"Who's that?" Pep and Rally asked in unison.

"Those trees have Murray Smith and John Assaraf on them. They started onecoach.com. Through this service, many small businesses have reached their own full potential. Assaraf is also a part of the well-known phenomenon, *The Secret*.

Eager Beaver looked around. "Over there is Maurice Martin."

"I've never heard of him," Pep said
Andre Agassi

"He started a company called iRise. Just as concept cars are made before they go into production, Maurice envisioned a product that would allow software companies to test drive their products before spending money and time on development. You may not know his company but his innovation will lower the cost of many products you buy.

"And speaking of cars," Eager Beaver pointed to the tree next to Maurice's. "Maurice knew Emmet B. Keeffe III for 18 months before the two men partnered and built iRise to become a $1 billion a year company. Emmet is probably the most connected person in the software industry. While he knows this business, Emmet's true passion is auto racing. When he's not working with iRise, he is involved in PKV Racing, a Champ Car World Series racing team."

"Cool," Pep and Rally chorused.

"Many people reach their own full potential by helping others reach theirs," Eager Beaver said. "Here is a better example."

Pep and Rally looked at the tree. "Who is that?"

"That is Karlheinz Brandenburg," Eager Beaver said.

"Karlheinz Brandenburg?" asked Pep.

"Karlheinz Brandenburg?" asked Rally.

"Who is Karlheinz Brandenburg?" they asked in unison.

"Do you still listen to music on vinyl disks?" asked Eager Beaver.

Karlhenz Brandenburg

"No," Pep laughed.

"Or even cassette tapes?"

"No," Rally said. "I have an MP3 player. I can download thousands of free songs from the Internet."

Eager Beaver gave Rally a stern look and slapped her tail. In response, Rally examined the way his fur fell over his belly. He knew he shouldn't be downloading songs without paying for them.

"Anyway," Eager Beaver continued, "Do you know who invented the MP3 player?"

"Karlheinz Brandenburg?" the rats asked.

"Yes, and you'll never hear about him. He came up with something that revolutionized how we listen to music and he will never receive personal credit for it. Instead, all the credit went to the committee he worked with and to the company he worked for.

"As important as taking control of your life is, it is just as important to share. We know about the trees of the major company leaders. But these leaders can't succeed without the right people supporting them. They need other people backing them and helping them to reach their full potential. This is how leaders support companies and their growth. Everyone within an organization needs to meet his or her full potential. That's what makes great companies great!

"So you can work for someone else and still reach your full potential?" Pep asked.

"Sure, millions of people do that every day," Eager Beaver replied. "We don't hear as much about them, but they are vital to the **Colleen Barrett** success of the companies they work for. You are confusing financial and business success with reaching your full potential. You must reach your full potential in everything you do. You must DARE to be the best citizen, parent, neighbor or person that you can be."

Eager Beaver looked around. "Look over there. She is a good example."

Pep and Rally looked up at the tree. "Who is she?" they asked in unison.

"This is Colleen Barrett," Eager Beaver said. "Her career began as a secretary at the law firm that helped Southwest Airlines get started in 1971. In 1978 she took a job as a corporate secretary at Southwest Airlines and worked her way up in the company. When the founder of Southwest Airlines retired, she became the president and chief operating officer of the company. That was three months before September 11, 2001. She quickly and successfully directed the effort to get Southwest Airlines flying again while reassuring customers that the airline was secure and safe. Today, when other airlines are struggling, Southwest Airlines continues to succeed. This success has been reached through a focus on customer service."

She pointed up at another tree.

"Another person with an airline who is very successful in other businesses as well is this man over here," continued Eager Beaver. "This is Sir Richard Branson who began with a small record shop and built an empire."

Riched Branson

"Do you know why his companies are called '*Virgin*'?" Eager Beaver asked.

"No," Pep said.

"No," Rally said.

"Why?" they asked in unison.

"When Sir Richard started his record label with his friends, one of the ladies said, 'We're all virgins at business'."

"Sir Richard took his relative lack of business knowledge and made his business into a success. Instead of remaining in the recording industry, Sir Richard shifted his focus to other enterprises, including the airline industry. He fought crushing competition from British Airways to start Virgin Airlines. Now, after years of fighting against US airline companies, he promises to reform the American airline industry too.

"Sir Richard is also known for his adventurous spirit. He attempts feats that haven't been done before, like crossing oceans in hot air balloons."

"Who is this?" Pep asked, wandering off to another tree.

"Oh, he's another innovator," said Eager Beaver. "It's Haim Saban. He's the one who started Power Rangers."

"I loved that show!" Rally yelled.

"Haim Saban is a recognized leader in the entertainment industry. As well as being the founder of Saban Entertainment and Fox Family Worldwide, Mr Saban is also a philanthropist

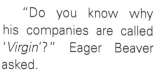

Hain Saban

and political activist with a focus on the US/Israeli relationship. Saban was born in Alexandria, Egypt in 1944. His family left their wartorn country when Sabian was 12 and moved to Israel. There, he eventually built the country's top tour promotion business. In 1975 Saban moved to France and built one of the most successful European labels in the recording industry. In 1983, he moved to Los Angeles where he built a chain of recording studios and rapidly became the top supplier of music for television.

"In 1988, Saban switched gears from music to television with the formation of Saban Entertainment, an international television, production, distribution and merchandising company. Saban Entertainment produced several major hits such as *X-Men*, numerous Marvel characters and the global phenomenon Mighty Morphin Power Rangers which to this day are the number one selling boys' toys in the United States.

"In 1997, the Saban-Fox partnership acquired the Fox Family Channel, a fully distributed cable network reaching 81 million homes. The company, known as Fox Family Worldwide, included the Fox Family Channel, the Fox Kids Network, Saban Entertainment, and Fox Kids International Network, a publicly traded European-based company with cable and satellite networks reaching 53 countries in

Kiyosaki

Europe and the Middle East. Unparalleled breadth and diversity of programming and an extraordinary global distribution platform means they were able to reach over 250 million homes worldwide. After deciding to dedicate a bigger portion of his time to his philanthropic and political activities, Mr Saban and Rupert Murdoch joined forces in the sale of Fox Family Worldwide to the Walt Disney Company. The deal, spearheaded by Mr Saban, was the largest cash transaction ever made by a single individual in the history of Hollywood. It closed on October 24, 2001. Mr Saban is not an overnight success though. Consistent hard work and recognizing his humble beginings have helped him achieve international success."

"I really like his story," said Pep.

"Me too," added Rally

"Tell us another good one, Eager," begged Pep.

"Okay, how about this person?" Eager Beaver asked, pointing to an image of a man wearing a turban.

"This is Mohammed bin Rashid Al Maktoum," said Eager Beaver. "This man is a visionary in the truest sense. As Prime Minister of the United Arab Emirates and Dubai's leader, Sheik Mohammed bin Rashid Al Maktoum has put his country on the world map as the most successful nation in the Middle East. Working first as a deputy to his father, the late Sheik Rashid,

Al Maktoum

and since 2006 ruling the country on his own, Sheik Mohammed has transformed the petroleum-poor desert emirate into a global center for business, finance, trade and tourism. He has laid the groundwork for success through his principles of modern development. Strong leadership, vision and innovation have made Sheikh Mohammed a synonym for success as he guides the people of Dubai, the United Arab Emirates and the Middle East towards a brighter future.

"His motivation for excellence makes him a role model for people around the world and he has contributed to many charitable causes. Most recently, in 2007, he set up the Mohammed bin Rashid al-Maktoum Foundation with a $10 billion endowment. Its purpose is to inspire knowledge, ideas and innovation among the builders of tomorrow's Arab world. He believes there needs to be a bridge between the Arab region and the developed world, improving the standard of education and research in the region, developing leadership programs for youth, and stimulating job creation. In 2007, he also launched a campaign, Dubai Cares, to raise money to educate 1 million children in poor countries. The campaign is Dubai's contribution to the UN Millennium Development Goals for providing Children's Primary Education to every child by 2015."

"Wow! There are so many people reaching their potential," said Rally, astounded by everything he was learning. He was beginning to feel more than a little inspired.

Riched Berman

Pep shifted his gaze. "Now, tell me, who's that?"

"Who *is* that guy?" Rally asked.

"Who?" Eager Beaver asked.

"Him," Pep and Rally said in unison.

Eager Beaver looked to where they were pointing. "That's Richard Berman. This is a man who preaches taking responsibility for your own decisions and actions. He grew up in New York City. His father ran gas stations and car washes. As a child, Berman worked summers and weekends to help his family make ends meet. He became a labor law attorney and worked for companies such as Bethlehem Steel and Dana Corporation before he became the labor law director of the US Chamber of Commerce."

Eager Beaver took a breath. "From there, he went into the food and beverage industry, eventually becoming an executive vice president at Pillsbury restaurant group. Berman became an advocate for taking responsibility. He manages the Center for Consumer Freedom, which argues that people should take responsibility for what they purchase and consume. But what's more controversial is that he manages the American Beverage Institute, which argues for societal tolerance of social drinking.

"While at times his message may be controversial, he does make a point that too often people blame others and eat the Bread of Shame," Eager Beaver said.

Pep nodded. He was beginning to understand what it meant to reach your full potential. Rally was thinking about the Bread of Shame. They each thought about Dreaming, Acting, Realizing and being Excited about life.

"D.A.R.E," they whispered in unison.

7

THE WISE OWL ARRIVES

As they moved further into the Forest of Hidden Potential, Pep and Rally noticed rocks lying on the ground. These weren't rocks typical of the ones you usually see in a forest. They were smooth river rocks. When Pep and Rally examined the rocks closely, they discovered that each one had writing on it.

"What are these?" Pep asked, picking up a rock.

"What's it say?" Rally asked.

"Alternative Fuel," they read.

Just as Pep turned to ask Eager Beaver about the meaning of words on the rock, a flutter of wings caught his attention.

"Yikes," he yelled.

Rally ducked. "Yikes," he yelled.

"Yikes," they yelled in unison as they scrambled to each find a hiding place.

"Pep! Rally! It's okay!" Eager Beaver called after them. "This is Richard, Richard the Wise Owl. He's not here to hurt you. He's here to guide and reveal to you the meaning of the Forest of Hidden Potential and D.A.R.E."

Pep and Rally stayed hidden, trembling with fear from the tops of their ears to the tips of their tails.

"Rats, I'm serious. Richard is my teacher. He oversees the Forest. It's from him that I have been taught about the Bread of Shame and how to apply D.A.R.E to my life. He taught me to **Dream**, to **Act**, to **Realize** my full potential, and to be **Excited** about life."

Pep peeked out from behind a rock.

Rally risked a look around a tree.

Richard the Wise Owl stood patiently waiting for them.

"Rats, don't be frightened," Eager Beaver tried again.

"Let me," Richard the Wise Owl said. Then he addressed the rats and said two words: "Blueberry Cheese."

"What?" asked Pep.

"What?" asked Rally.

They almost asked 'What?' in unison, but Richard the Wise Owl cut them off. "I said Blueberry Cheese."

They had never told ANYONE about the Blueberry Cheese they had planned to make.

"What's that about?" Eager Beaver asked.

"They know," said Richard the Wise Owl and nodded at Pep and Rally.

Slowly, Pep slid out from behind the rock. Rally carefully shifted from the back of the tree. They stood facing Richard the Wise Owl while staying a safe distance from his talons. They were going to avoid being an owl's meal at all costs.

"You were wondering about the rocks," Richard the Wise Owl said. "These are all the ideas, actions, possibilities and potentials that were wasted by people. Maybe they died before they could reach their full potential or maybe they just ate the Bread of Shame and forgot their **Dreams**, failed to take **Action**, never **Realized** their full potential or lacked **Excitement** about life. When that happens, their hidden potential comes here to the Forest of Hidden Potential. The potential is carved on a rock and awaits someone else who is worthy and ready. And sometimes, just sometimes, it is the same person."

Richard the Wise Owl picked up a rock. "Here," he said. "You might find this one fascinating."

Pep looked at Rally.

Rally looked at Eager Beaver. Pep took a deep breath and moved one more step towards Richard the Wise Owl. Meanwhile, Rally scurried over and grabbed the rock from Richard the Wise Owl and retreated to a safe distance.

"What is it?" Pep asked as he scuttled over to Rally.

Rally examined the rock and held it out for Pep. "Blueberry Cheese," they read aloud.

"It looks like it has a hinge," Pep said as he pointed to the rock.

Rally examined it in detail. He found a latch and opened the rock. Inside it he found a card. On the card was the recipe for Blueberry Cheese. Pep and Rally both gasped.

Richard the Wise Owl motioned to Eager Beaver, who walked over and took the card and rock back from the rats.

Richard the Wise Owl said, "You had the potential to make Blueberry Cheese. That recipe was in you all this time. You even began taking the right steps towards realizing your full potential. You knew you needed more knowledge to be successful at making Blueberry Cheese, so you started by working at The Little Cheese Company.

"Unfortunately, while you were there, you were diverted from your true potential. Instead, you began eating the Bread of Shame and failed to reach your full potential. Then, when Big Cheese Incorporated bought The Little Cheese Company, it didn't need workers like you, so you were laid off.

"That would have been the perfect time to begin making Blueberry Cheese. But the two of you continued to feast on the Bread of Shame. Day after day, you wasted opportunities to get off your duffs and make your own @#$! cheese. And finally that potential made its way back to the Forest of Hidden Potential where it waits for more worthy and ready creatures."

"But ..." Pep started.

"But ..." Rally started.

"But ..." they both said again.

"Oh, you never really lost your potential. You can still achieve your true potential. But you must be a cause in your lives instead of playing the victim and simply reacting to things as they come to you. You need to creatively pursue your true potential, take control of your life, and finally, you must share with others. Only then will you achieve your full potential."

"But ..." Pep started.

"But ..." Rally started.

"But ..." they both said again.

"You have a question, Rally," Richard the Wise Owl observed.

"Well," Rally paused and looked at Eager Beaver. "What about Eager? She works for Big Cheese. She hasn't made her own @#$! cheese."

"Yeah," Pep said.

Richard the Wise Owl smiled to himself. "Eager continues to strive to reach her full potential. Her full potential is to be the best employee of Big Cheese Incorporated she can be. Her full potential was never to go out on her own and start her own business. Her full potential is to support her children, her community and the company for which she works.

"Every day, Eager goes to work excited about reaching her full potential for the day. She makes her own @#$! cheese every day as she pours over reports, manages others and makes sure her department stays under budget. She is always looking for ways to help Big Cheese Incorporated grow, expand and prosper.

"At home, Eager carefully saves her money and takes care of her family. Her full potential is also reached through frugality. Unlike you rats who could have become wealthy by making a superior cheese that everyone wanted, Eager's wealth will come from dedication, wise and careful investments and money management.

"You mean we still have a chance?" Pep asked.

"You always have potential, as long as you're alive," Richard the Wise Owl said.

Dane Cook

"Really?" Rally asked.

"Really," Richard the Wise Owl said. "Every day, you must Dream, Act, Realize and be Excited. You must reverse the effects of eating the Bread of Shame by sharing and giving back. You need to go back and help others who deserve to be helped. You must tell them about D.A.R.E and help them to reach their full potential.

"Of course, it also takes hard work and dedication," Richard the Wise Old Owl added knowingly. "People are always looking for the easy way but achieving your full potential takes dedication and hard work.

"For instance, have you ever heard of Dane Cook?"

"Yes," Pep and Rally said in unison.

"I used to download clips of his shows from his website at work," Pep said before he thought about what he was admitting to. He looked quickly at Eager Beaver's tail, expecting it to slap the ground but thankfully, it stayed where it was.

Rally had a little more time to think about what he was going to say. "He's my favorite comedian."

Richard the Wise Owl said, "Dane didn't just go out to comedy clubs and tell a few jokes, he dedicated himself to reaching his full potential.

"Even at a young age, Dane Cook had a talent for comedy. He was fortunate to have a supportive family who encouraged him to develop his talents. His father bought him a tape recorder and Dane began practicing the routines of great comedians.

"When his career was finally developing, Dane knew that to reach his full potential he needed to do something other comedians hadn't done before. He took all of his savings — he even cashed in his retirement accounts — and built the best website money could buy. That is how much he believed in himself and his potential."

"Wow," Pep and Rally said, thinking about how they hadn't invested a dime in their idea of Blueberry Cheese. They had taken a job to learn the business, but that wasn't much of a sacrifice.

"Later," Richard the Wise Owl continued, "when he saw the power of social networking websites, Dane Cook not only created his own profile, like so many other people have done, but he dedicated himself to updating it regularly, offering content to his visitors and creating an extensive friends list.

"Dane didn't do things the way other comics had done them. He found a unique path to his full potential and he invested everything he had — time, effort and money — into ways of reaching his full potential.

"But he didn't stop there. Dane also gave back. He is known for being accessible to his fans, meeting with them after his shows and signing autographs until the last one is signed. He also attempts to answer every email people send him which is getting more difficult the more famous he becomes.

"Instead of basking in his own success, Dane also supports other people and their careers. When HBO wanted to sponsor *Tourgasm*, they didn't want the other comedians on the program. Most people would have accepted HBO's offer, especially since it was such a great opportunity, but Dane defended himself to HBO, saying he would rather pay for the tour himself than send the other comedians away. HBO gave in to Dane and sponsored the tour.

"The keys to Dane's success are his tireless dedication to reaching his full potential and his willingness to give back to those who have helped him to reach his full potential. Too often, people fail on both fronts. They either sit back and wait for fortune to find them, or, when they do become successful, they often become content to take the money and praise from others without giving back. You two would do well to learn from Dane Cook's example," Richard the Wise Owl said.

Pep and Rally nodded. They had never thought about the path that brought success to others. It just seemed like they were fortunate enough to have found themselves at the right place at the right time.

Richard the Wise Owl gestured around the Forest of Hidden Potential. "Look around. Out of all those rocks, only one has the recipe for Blueberry Cheese. Together the two of you have a unique potential and you must dedicate yourselves to reaching that potential. In doing so, you should also remember to give back."

Richard the Wise Owl pointed to a rock. "This is the rock of an individual who read a book about making your own @#$! cheese and did nothing about it. Instead of inventing a renewable source of energy, she continued eating the Bread of Shame."

Pep, Rally and Eager Beaver looked at each other.

"But that book hasn't been written yet," Pep said.

"That's because the potential author only dreamed about writing the book. He never dedicated the time or resources necessary for the book to be written. Now it finds itself here as a rock in the Forest of Hidden Potential.

"When people do reach their potential, these rocks become theirs. Eventually, someone else will make Blueberry Cheese if the two of you keep eating the Bread of Shame and continue to be distracted from reaching your full potential.

"We are all connected. If Blueberry Cheese is not made, someone else will not be able to reach his or her full potential. A better example would be the personal computer. If it had not been invented, it could not have been refined. And if it hadn't been refined, it would not have supported Bill Gates' software. In other words, Gates could not have reached his full potential if someone else had not reached theirs."

"Hmm," Rally said.

"Right," Eager Beaver nodded.

"Uh huh," Pep agreed.

"In fact," Richard the Wise Owl said, "Mr Gates' tree is right over there. He had a cushy beginning which is rare in the Forest of Hidden Potential. Living off your family's wealth is eating the Bread of Shame. It is unfortunate that wealthy parents often hook their children on to the Bread of Shame at a young age.

Bill Gates

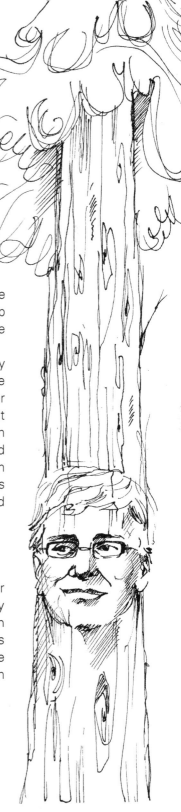

"Fortunately, Gates did not eat the Bread of Shame, even though he was born with a million-dollar trust fund. Instead, he strove to reach his full potential every day. He used his early access to computers to learn everything he could about technology. Then he launched a career of defining the personal computer. It all started when he helped his high school computerize its payroll. And now most of the world uses some form of Microsoft's software.

"Gates has stepped down from the day-to-day operations of Microsoft to focus more of his time on giving to others through the Bill and Melinda Gates Foundation. We can expect some amazing things to come as they work to help others reach their full potential."

The pair nodded their heads in unison, trying to absorb everything they had learned from Eager Beaver and Richard the Wise Owl.

"Think about what you've learned here today," Richard the Wise Owl said. "Remember, you can return to the Forest of Hidden Potential whenever you want; however, Eager Beaver has given you a gift that you must pass on. You won't be able to return here until you have truly given to others in a similar fashion."

"But we could keep all these ideas for ourselves," Pep said.

Richard the Wise Owl blinked. "You cannot. There is the reality of the forest. Coming back here while eating the Bread of Shame will never work. You won't see the faces in the trees and you won't be able to read these rocks.

"In the meantime, I will keep this Blueberry Cheese recipe here safely for the two of you. When you are ready, you can return and retrieve it. I will be waiting."

"Thank you, Richard," Pep said.

"Thank you, Richard," Rally said.

"Thanks again, Richard," Eager Beaver added.

"All of you are welcome. I hope you visit me again soon."

With that, Richard the Wise Owl flew off.

"Wow," Pep said.

"Yeah, wow," Rally said.

"We better get started," Pep said.

"You bet," Rally said.

Eager Beaver joined the rats as they skipped back down the path towards her car.

Eager Beaver and the Wise Owl opened Pep and Rally's eyes to their behavior at The Little Cheese Company. Pep and Rally had forgotten their reason for wanting to work for the company in the first place. They had taken advantage of their employer for the free lunch and other benefits instead of seeking knowledge by taking a closer look into the departments they were auditing and by assisting their colleagues. They were not living up to their full potential. They understood now why Eager Beaver wasn't laid off but promoted instead. She lived up to her full potential as the best employee of Big Cheese Incorporated. She worked hard at her current job and contributed to the growth of the company by offering to help in other departments and volunteering her time to the various community programs with which The Little Cheese Company was involved. Go to www.MakeYourOwnDamnCheese.com and see more stories about individuals who live up to their full potential every day and how more and more companies are putting an emphasis on giving back.

8

PEP AND RALLY GET OFF THEIR DUFFS

What did Pep and Rally do after their field trip with Eager Beaver? They were inspired to finally get off their duffs and begin working on making their own @#$! cheese.

The following morning, they woke up at 7:30 and behaved as if they were going to work which, in fact, they were. But they were now working for Top Cheese Incorporated, the name they had decided on for their own company. They met at 8:30 at the kitchen table and began laying out a strategy and timetable so that they could meet their ultimate goal. As they marked off on the calendar what they wanted to achieve, and by when they wanted to achieve it, Pep noticed something. "Hey, Rally?"

"Yeah, Pep?"

"Isn't Chinese New Year coming up?"

"Um, I don't know."

"I think it's some time after our New Year," Pep said.

"Then I guess it is," Rally said, not understanding what that had to do with their plans.

"What is the Chinese animal for next year?"

"I have no idea," said Rally, who, while he knew a lot about cheese, knew very little about Chinese astrology.

"We should Google it to find out, just in case," Pep said.

"Just in case of what?" Rally asked.

"Just in case it's an auspicious year."

"Oh yeah, an auspicious year," Rally nodded his head, although he wasn't all that sure what 'auspicious' meant in the first place.

Pep didn't notice Rally's confusion. Instead, he was already exploring different websites. "Aha, there it is, the Year of the Rat. I told you it would be auspicious."

Since Rally wasn't sure if that was a good thing or a bad thing, he asked, "What's it say?"

"It says the Year of the Rat is a time for hard work. It is a good time to begin a new job or launch a new product. See, this *is* an auspicious year," Pep said.

"Ah, yes, an auspicious year," Rally said. Reading on, Pep summarized: "It's a good time to make a fresh start. Ventures begun this year will yield fast returns. That sounds good."

"Yes, auspicious," Rally said.

"What else? We need to be prepared, which we are, and patient," Pep read ahead. "It says this will be an adventuresome year with material rewards."

"I like that," Rally said.

"We better get started then. We can't waste another day," Pep said.

"We better get started right away," Rally agreed.

"Let's get started!" they said in unison.

And so they did. They began by cleaning their apartment. They then organized the dining room and living room to look more like an office than living quarters. But most importantly, they threw out all the bread. They resolved to eat only cheese or die of starvation. Pep and Rally understood that pain can sometimes be a great motivator. They knew they could no longer put off until tomorrow what should have been accomplished yesterday.

On Tuesday, Pep and Rally visited Harry's apartment. Harry hadn't done very well for himself since the Big Cheese Incorporated acquisition. Pep and Rally described to him their plan for making their own cheese and told Harry how he could contribute as an accountant. Since Harry had nothing else to do other than watch television all day, he decided to help out.

On Wednesday, Irene was inspired by Pep and Rally's enthusiasm. She agreed to spearhead the marketing department. She set to work on the new company's strategic marketing plan.

It took a little more persuasion to get Jonathan on board than it did the previous two. He heard Pep and Rally's enthusiasm but, as a more rational and calculating creature, he needed to read their plan and consider the feasibility of their strategy and timetable.

After meeting with Pep and Rally on Thursday morning, Jonathan spoke with Harry about the numbers and with Irene about the marketability of Blueberry Cheese. At the end of the day, Jonathan agreed to be in charge of purchasing all the necessary equipment. He researched stocking issues, over-runs, buy-backs and risk management. Kristen had spent so much time interviewing for jobs that she felt she would make a great director of creature relations. She wanted to make sure that Pep and Rally's company took care of its team members.

By Friday afternoon, Pep and Rally only needed to talk to one other person. No one had heard from Leslie since the layoffs. When they asked around, they heard rumors that Leslie was in prison. Evidently things had gotten so difficult for her that she had become involved in money scams.

"Do you think a person in prison can reach her full potential?" Pep asked Rally.

"How can you get off your duff and make your own @#$! cheese behind bars?" Rally asked Pep.

They each thought about it.

"Martha Stewart went to prison and continued to build an empire. And she has a tree in the Forest of Potential," Pep recalled.

Maratha Stewart

"Michael Milken was wealthier after prison than before," Rally said.

"Don King," Pep added.

"What about Nelson Mandela?" Rally said triumphantly. "He really used his time in prison to reach his full potential."

"Let's call Leslie," they said in unison.

And they did. Leslie was surprised to hear they wanted her on board but quickly agreed to help Irene write some of the marketing material.

The rest of team worked on their business plan over the weekend. By Monday, they were ready to visit some banks for a loan. The First Cheese Bank turned them down. Wisconsin Cheese Bank turned them down. The Bank of Cheese turned them down. Even the Cheese Credit Union wouldn't give them the time of day. The Cheese Bank and Trust explained to them how they would fail. Cheese Savings and Loans gave them forms to fill out, but refused to meet with them.

By the end of the week, Harry, Irene, Jonathan and Kristen were discouraged, but Pep and Rally were ready to rethink their approach.

Pep addressed the group. "Listen, rats, walls are really hurdles. They can be jumped over, dug under or broken through. They don't have to stop us in our tracks."

"What did the Google guys do when they needed to move their project from a class assignment to become the leading search engine?" Rally asked. "They were only graduate students, so they needed a lot of money to make Google work."

"That's right," Pep said. "Eager told us they raised their initial $1.1 million from investors who understood the power of their search engine."

"That's right," Rally said, "We need to find investors who understand the value of Blueberry Cheese."

"Hey, remember Kelly Perdew?" Pep asked.

"Oh yeah," Rally said.

"Who's that?" Kristen asked.

"Have you ever watched *The Apprentice* on TV?" Pep asked.

"No," Harry, Irene, Jonathan and Kristen said in unison.

"Evidently there were some important lessons about reaching your full potential in the show," Rally said. "We didn't see the show either, but we wish we had. Maybe we wouldn't have sat around eating the Bread of Shame."

"Anyway," Pep continued, "Kelly Perdew won in the show's second season. He had a successful academic and military career prior to appearing. He also received a Presidential Appointment to the Council of Service and Civic Participation from President George W. Bush."

"But most importantly, after working with Donald Trump Perdew began to manage a prestigious venture capital fund."

Jonathan cut in. "Do you think we could get a hold of him to invest in our cheese factory?"

"Maybe," Pep said. "Eager might be able to introduce us through *GotAccess*."

"Hooray," the rats cheered.

"We need to find investors who will help us reach our dreams," Rally said.

"Blueberry Cheese investors," everyone said in unison.

Pep and Rally visited Eager Beaver. They gave her their business plan and asked if she could help them shop it around to investors she knew through her network. Meanwhile, the other rats got on the phone and began making visits to other possible investors.

While searching for investors, they also toured shut-down cheese factories. As it turned out, one factory had been abandoned. It was the perfect size and included the equipment they needed to add non-milk ingredients to the cheese. The factory had made boursin cheese with herbs, garlic and

Howard Schult

other additives. It would be a simple task to modify the equipment to accommodate blueberries. Jonathan got right to work making the modifications.

Now they could visualize their Blueberry Cheese operation.

"Remember the law of attraction?" Pep asked his friend. "What you think about, you bring about."

"Right," Rally said. "We should tell everyone about Howard Schultz."

"Who is that?" Harry asked.

"Remember how much coffee we drank at The Little Cheese Company?" Rally asked.

"Coffee?" Jonathan asked.

"The gourmet coffee we had in the break room?" Kristen asked.

"Yep, that coffee came to us courtesy of Howard Schultz," Pep said with a smile.

"Starbucks," they said in unison.

"Yup," Pep said. "Schultz had humble beginnings. He grew up in federally subsidized housing in Brooklyn, New York. But he refused to eat the Bread of Shame."

"That's right," Rally broke in. "He worked hard in school and became the first person in his family to graduate from college. When he started working for Starbucks, the company only sold coffee beans. But Howard had a dream of recreating Italian espresso bars in the United States. The management at Starbucks didn't see his vision, so Howard left to start Il Giornale. The original Starbucks company started working with Peet's Coffee and Tea and sold the name 'Starbucks' to Howard. Today, North Americans and people all over the world no longer drink freeze-dried coffee out of a can. Instead, they say they want a Starbucks when they want coffee."

"And this started with a vision of coffee bars. Shultz changed the way people drink coffee," Pep said.

"Let's visualize our cheese plant and before you know it, we'll be making Blueberry Cheese," Rally said.

"Hooray!" they all cheered unison.

And this is exactly what happened. By the end of the week, they had enough financing from different sources to begin operations. Once they had this money, the banks that had originally turned them down were now eager to be a part of the business. The rats had enough capital to give each team member a paycheck and to make their company official. Before they knew it, they were ready to start making, marketing and selling Blueberry Cheese.

"Okay, where's the recipe?" Harry asked.

Pep looked at Rally. "How would you rats like to go for a picnic?" he asked.

"But we have so much to do," Irene complained.

"We'll go this Sunday," Rally said. "We have someone we want you to meet."

"Who?" Jonathan asked.

"Richard the Wise Owl," Pep said.

"In the Forest of Hidden Potential," Rally piped up.

There was a pause.

"What are you rats doing hanging out with owls?" Kristen asked.

"What are you doing hanging out in the Forest of Hidden Potential?" Harry asked incredulously.

"Didn't you guys read the sign?" Irene nearly shrieked.

"Why, yes we did," Pep said.

"We did indeed," Rally said.

"Huh," Jonathan grunted.

Kristen shivered in fear.

However, that Sunday the whole crew went to the Forest of Hidden Potential. Along the way, Pep and Rally explained the meaning of D.A.R.E, the Bread of Shame, and even the rocks that littered the Forest of Hidden Potential.

"Hey Harry, check it out," Pep called.

"Who's that?" Harry asked looking up at the tree Pep was pointing to.

"Who's that carved into the tree?" Irene asked

"As a kid, he liked sweets almost as much as Harry does," Rally told them.

"But look at what a physique he developed," Pep said.

Jonathan came over. "Who is it?"

"That," said Rally, "is Jack Lalanne. Some know him as the juice man. But long before he was popular, he was a body builder and nutrition expert."

"When he was young, he was a very angry person. He tried to burn his family's house down," Pep said.

"But when he heard a lecture on health, he began eating better and lifting weights. He became known for his great feats of strength," Rally said. "For instance, when he was 60 he swam from Alcatraz to San Francisco with his hands cuffed behind his back, his legs shackled and towing a thousand-foot boat."

"And he helped others by opening fitness gyms and producing exercise shows on television," Pep said. "He inspired many people to live healthier lives."

"Amazing," Kristen said.

"How about this person?" asked Irene. "He looks familiar."

"That's Mark Cubin," said Rally. "I know his story."

"In 1983, soon after graduating from Indiana University, Mark Cuban founded his own computer consulting firm, MicroSolutions Inc. After seven years of non-stop work, the company became hugely successful and Cuban agreed to sell it to CompuServe. This venture made Cuban a millionaire and an early retiree.

"While reminiscing with a friend in his new hometown of Dallas about the good old days at Indiana University, Cuban wished he could hear a Hoosiers games on the radio. This led to his next brilliant idea — broadcasting radio and TV on the Internet. With that, Broadcast.com was born. The result? Cuban became a major player in multimedia.

"In January 2000, this sports fan decided to attack a new realm of business. He purchased his hometown basketball team, the Dallas Mavericks, for an estimated $285 million. The image of the organization improved immediately. Games the Mavericks played in were soon known for having a more positive atmosphere and contagious energy than other NBA games.

"This stems from Cuban's ability to instill pride and passion into fans. He is the first owner in any team sport who encourages fan interaction through email on his own personal computer. Cuban himself has replied to thousands of emails. Cuban has shown the Mavericks his commitment to seeing them win. And in return, this is exactly what they've done.

"To add to his incredible feats with the Mavericks, Cuban started a high-definition TV network called HDNet in 2001. Carrying sports, movies and quality programming, the channels represent the wave of HDTV that is storming living rooms across the world. Cuban even has his own sports show filmed in the team's home arena, the American Airlines Center.

"In addition to owning the Mavericks, Cuban is an active investor in cutting-edge technologies and continues to be a sought-after speaker," said Rally.

"Another excellent example," said Pep. "Well done, Rally."

"This place is so inspiring," said Harry.

As promised, Richard the Wise Owl met the party among the trees. The other rats hid behind Pep and Rally who were no longer afraid of Richard the Wise Owl's talons.

"Here you go," Richard the Wise Owl said, as he handed Pep and Rally the rock with 'Blueberry Cheese' written on it.

Pep quickly opened the rock. Rally took out the recipe for Blueberry Cheese and showed it to the other rats.

"Hooray!" they all yelled in unison.

Richard the Wise Owl smiled and said, "I've got something else to show you."

He led the group through the trees to a tree with a new facade on it. The new bark shone in the light filtering through the forest. Everyone in the group gasped when they recognized Eager Beaver.

"Hooray!" cheered Pep.

"Hooray!" cheered Rally.

"Hooray!" they all cheered. It was a wonderful day.

One month later, the first batch of Blueberry Cheese rolled out of the production line. Initially, demand was limited, but soon interest started growing. Stores were putting blueberry cheese on their shelves. People were ordering quantities over the Internet. And a few magazines came to tour the plant and write articles about the wonders of Blueberry Cheese. It received rave reviews.

People were intrigued by the interesting policy Top Cheese Incorporated had. Most cheese factories offered free samples. But Top Cheese Inc gave nothing out for free. If you didn't want to pay for a sample of Blueberry Cheese, you could ask to perform some other task, such as cleaning up the sampling area. You could also donate to a variety of charities. Those wanting volume discounts were asked to volunteer in their communities to receive the discounts.

Furthermore, the acronym D.A.R.E. was printed on the back of every brochure, advertisement and flyer for Top Cheese Inc. Pep and Rally were only too happy to tell people what it meant when they were asked.

Six months later, Top Cheese Inc was so busy they couldn't keep up with demand. They had to raise prices to slow demand while they expanded. Shortly thereafter, Eager Beaver visited.

"Hey, Eager," Pep said, rushing out to hug Eager Beaver. "Hey, Rally, look who's here!"

"Hey, Eager," Rally said as he ran around his desk to embrace her.

"How have you been, Eager?" Pep asked.

"Great," Eager Beaver said. "And you guys?"

"Great," Pep said.

"Great," Rally echoed.

"Wonderful," Eager Beaver said. "Actually, I'm here on business."

"Business?" Pep asked.

"Yes, you see, I'm now a vice president at Big Cheese Incorporated and we are interested in acquiring your company."

Pep and Rally looked at each other.

"Well," Pep said.

"We'll have to discuss it," Rally said.

"Plus, we are employee owned," Pep said.

"Oh, we know all of that," Eager Beaver said. "I think you'll like the terms we're offering."

And they did. Not only did Pep and Rally agree, but Harry, Irene, Jonathan and Kristen also gave their approval. Even though Leslie had six months left of her prison term, she too agreed to the terms of the acquisition.

Not only did Pep and Rally make a lot of money in the sale of their company, they also accepted positions on the board of Big Cheese Incorporated. With their extra time and new positions, they began telling other people about the Forest of Hidden Potential.

Postscript

And so this story ends, but the story of Pep, Rally, the other rats and Eager Beaver continues. Each one reaches his or her full potential by waking up each morning with a **Dream**. They take **Action** each day to realize their dream, thus **Realizing** their true potential. And best of all, they are **Excited** about living a great life.

You can learn more about their success and the success of other people who are reaching their full potential at www. MakeYourOwnDamnCheese.com. At that website you can also nominate someone you know who is reaching his or her full potential for our monthly Forest of Hidden Potential award.

Printed in Australia
AUOC02n1146290914
263468AU00004B/5/P